HOMEMADE DOLLS
in FOREIGN DRESS

by the same author

THE HOME TOY SHOP

HOLIDAY HANDICRAFT

HOMEMADE DOLLS
in Foreign Dress

by NINA R. JORDAN

ILLUSTRATED BY THE AUTHOR

HARCOURT, BRACE AND COMPANY
NEW YORK

PRINTED IN THE UNITED STATES OF AMERICA

*To Bob and Sarah
this book is lovingly dedicated
by the author*

INTRODUCTION

WHAT ARE THEY, DOLLS?

In a way, yes, but they are far more than dolls. They are miniature people of different foreign nations, and you can make them
yourself together with the homes they live in and some of the
things they use. They are almost as flexible as you are. They are
sturdy, too, when well made.

BUT AREN'T THEY HARD TO MAKE?

Indeed not, they are very simply made. Look at the illustrations
that show their construction, and you'll see that this is true.

YES, BUT THE AUTHOR IS AN EXPERT AND I'M NOT

But the author is new at this doll-making, too! Until five months
before this book was written she had never made one of these dolls.
We began with experiments on which we tried out different kinds
of wires and different ways of constructing. The stiff wire we used
at first made strong but rigid dolls. The soft copper wire which we
now use makes the dolls flexible and is stiff enough because of the
tight wrappings of stocking strips. These add strength but retain
the flexibility.

When we had finally succeeded in working out this simple way of making strong flexible dolls, we made up the models you see illustrated here. So you might say that the author is really an amateur who is barely a few jumps ahead of the beginners.

On those experimental dolls we made every blunder that anyone could possibly make, so now we can help you avoid our mistakes. We will also explain how to remedy the mistakes that you may make. For this reason your first doll can't help being much better than our first two or three were.

And yet, though our first attempts were not much to look at, we were fond of them from the very start. It is amazing to behold bare wires and old stockings turn into little people who smile at you with their painted mouths and twinkle at you with their bright bead eyes. You'll get a thrill, too, when you see this thing happen under your own fingers.

These homemade manikins have several unusual qualities. One is the few and simple materials that make them—mere twists of stocking over pieces of wire. Another is the ease with which they are made.

But their most remarkable feature is their ability to take and hold human poses. They don't just stand stiffly like dolls—they are always doing things.

The arms and legs can be bent into any human position. The hands can grasp and hold things. The body, too, can be bent in almost any way that our own bodies bend. Only the head is at all stationary but even it can be adjusted somewhat.

Our drawings, made from the actual models, show only a few of the ways in which these little figures can be kept busy. They are a nice size, too—about eight inches—therefore their costumes require but the merest scraps of material.

The manikins can be made to stand on such simply made bases as we have illustrated.

There have been dolls of some kind almost as long as there have been people in the world to love them. Whenever and wherever people have wanted to make dolls, they have always found materials with which to make them. Dolls have been made of bone, ivory, and wood, of seaweed and shells, of plaster, wax, china, and cloth. Eskimos and American Indians make dolls of leather stuffed with moss or grass, and Mexicans make them of corn husks.

All of us are familiar with children's dolls of rubber, rags, yarn, and paper, and with the unbreakable dolls made of paper and paste. And to this list let us now add our agile new doll with its stocking skin and its wire bones.

Nor are children the only ones who love dolls. There are thousands of adults—both men and women—who make doll-collecting a hobby.

Among the varieties of dolls valued by collectors are costume dolls in the fascinating dress of far-away lands, and it is with this kind of doll that our book is concerned.

The making of one of our dolls requires only an old stocking, a piece of wire and some cotton.

Although we often call our manikins "dolls" (because "dolls" is such a nice short word) they are really tiny people living in a midget world of their own, since we have also provided homes and familiar surroundings for them.

So here they are, lively and ready for anything. And—best of all—they are all yours for the making.

TABLE OF CONTENTS

HOMEMADE DOLLS
in FOREIGN DRESS

MAKING THE DOLLS

MATERIALS FOR MAKING THE DOLLS:

A spool of No. 18 copper wire (25-foot spool at Woolworth's costs 10¢). This wire is soft enough to be bent
with your fingers.

Tie wire (a 30-foot spool costs 5¢ at Dennison's).

Old stockings.

Cotton (a 10¢ package).

Pliers with a wire-cutting slot (Woolworth stores have
them).

Needle and thread.

STOCKINGS. All the doll figures in this book may be
made with stockings of four colors: black, light flesh color,
medium tan, and dark tan. By medium tan we mean about
the color of wrapping paper. Dark tan is about the color of
coffee with very little cream in it.

Light flesh color makes Swedish, Dutch, Swiss, and
Scotch dolls.

Medium tan makes the Chinese, Japanese, French, and
Italian dolls.

Dark tan is used for Mexican, Eskimo, Arab, South
American, Hindu, and Pueblo Indian dolls.

Black is for the African.

Stockings should be smoothly pressed out for easy
handling. Chiffon stockings are not the best material—
they are difficult to cut because of their flimsiness. But
they can be used for stuffing the body.

The easiest stocking material to work with is soft lisle
or cotton, though silk may be used, of course.

MAKING HEAD AND BODY. First, cut off the hem
and foot of the stocking. If the hem is double, open it out
and use it for the doll's head and body.

Stuff the head and body with cotton or with pieces of silk
stockings. The illustration shows the shape of the head and
body and how they are made. The body may be rather
loosely stuffed, but the head should be firm and just about
the size of a golf ball. Before tying it at the neck, poke the

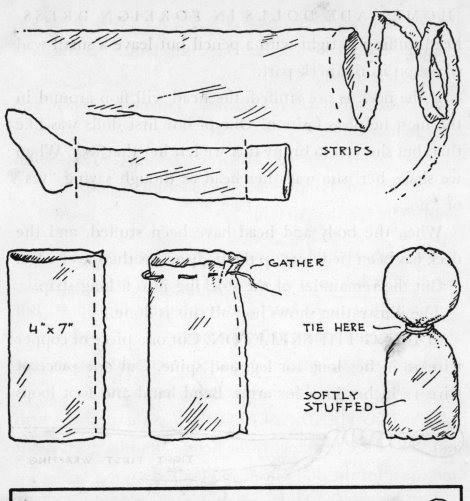

STRIPS

GATHER

4"x7"

TIE HERE

SOFTLY STUFFED

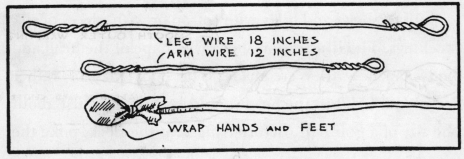

LEG WIRE 18 INCHES
ARM WIRE 12 INCHES

WRAP HANDS and FEET

head stuffing in tight with a pencil but leave a small wad of cotton in the neck part.

If the neck is not stuffed, the head will flop around in the most helpless fashion! One of our first dolls was like that, but she was so funny that we left her that way. When we shake her, she wags her head as though saying "yes" or "no."

When the body and head have been stuffed, and the neck has been tied, sew up the body across the lower edge.

Cut the remainder of the stocking into a long strip.

The illustration shows how all this is done.

MAKING THE SKELETON. Cut one piece of copper wire 18 inches long for legs and spine. Cut one piece of wire 12 inches long for arms. Bend hand and foot loops

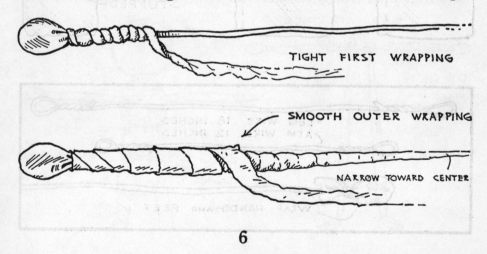

TIGHT FIRST WRAPPING

SMOOTH OUTER WRAPPING

NARROW TOWARD CENTER

at the ends. After loops are bent, the arm wire should measure 8 inches long and the leg wire about 15 inches.

Cover the end loops with bits of stocking, tied or sewed firmly. Then cover the remainder of the wires. The first strips of stocking to go around the wires should be wound just as tight as you can wind them. This causes the strip to roll up and form crosswise ridges, as you see in the illustration.

Next you add a smooth second covering, wound less tightly and caught with stitches to keep it snug.

After these coverings are on, bend the long leg wire into two legs and bind the arm and leg wires together at their centers to form a skeleton. (See illustration.)

Then join the wire skeleton to the stuffed body. Place

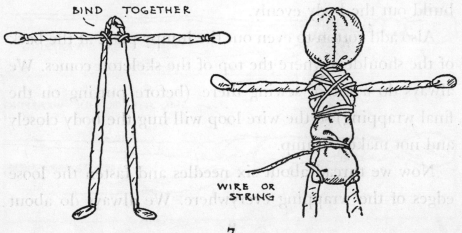

BIND TOGETHER

WIRE OR
STRING

the skeleton against the back of the body and be careful to keep the lower part of the padded body BETWEEN the leg wires. Tie it there, and sew it there, too, so it will stay that way.

Make the tie-wire wrappings tight around the body, going sometimes around, sometimes diagonally, as the illustration shows. Particularly at the shoulders are these diagonal wrappings important, for they are what keep the arms well fastened to the body. Use plenty of tie-wire—we never use less than two yards of it for this part of the construction.

Next, put on wrappings of stocking strips to smooth it all out and to give arms, legs, and body more bulk. Be sure to poke in a little cotton wherever it is needed to help build out the body evenly.

Also add cotton to even out the lumpy place at the back of the shoulders where the top of the skeleton comes. We always do a bit of sewing there (before putting on the final wrapping) so the wire loop will hug the body closely and not make a bump.

Now we thread about six needles and fasten the loose edges of the wrapping everywhere. We always do about

8

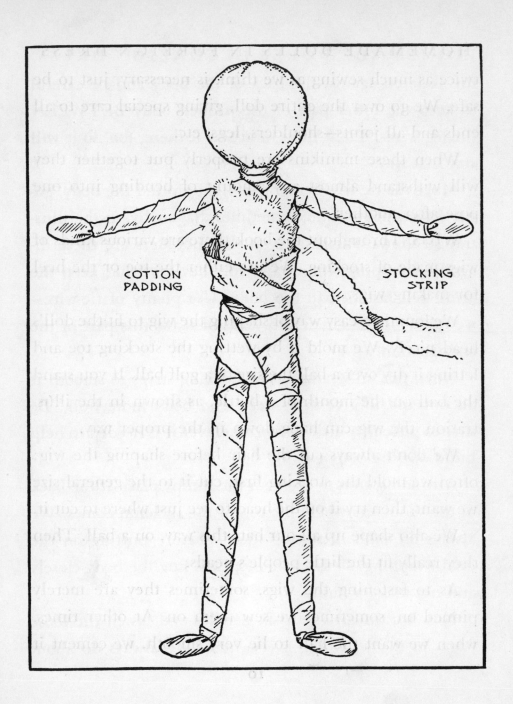

COTTON
PADDING

STOCKING
STRIP

twice as much sewing as we think is necessary, just to be safe. We go over the entire doll, giving special care to all ends and all joints—shoulders, legs, etc.

When these manikins are properly put together they will withstand almost any amount of bending into one pose after another.

WIGS. Throughout the book there are various kinds of wigs made of stocking. We use either the toe or the heel for making wigs.

We found an easy way of shaping the wig to fit the doll's head nicely. We mold it by wetting the stocking toe and letting it dry over a ball the size of a golf ball. If you stand the ball on the mouth of a bottle, as shown in the illustration, the wig can hang down in the proper way.

We don't always cut the hair before shaping the wig; often we mold the stocking first, cut it to the general size we want, then try it on the head to see just where to cut it.

We also shape up all our hats this way, on a ball. Then they really fit the little people's heads.

As to fastening the wigs, sometimes they are merely pinned on, sometimes we sew them on. At other times, when we want the hair to lie very smooth, we cement it

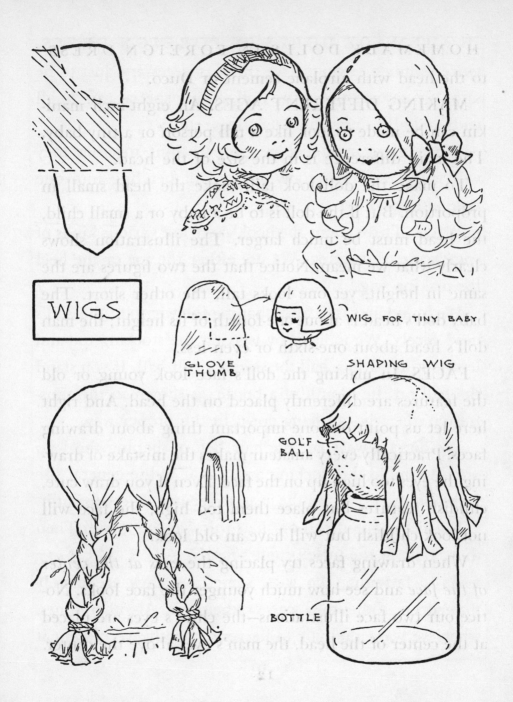

WIGS

GLOVE THUMB

WIG FOR TINY BABY

SHAPING WIG

GOLF BALL

BOTTLE

to the head with airplane cement or Duco.

MAKING DIFFERENT AGES. An eight-inch mani-
kin can be made to look like a tall person or a tiny baby.
The main difference is in the size of the head.

To make the doll look tall, make the head small in
proportion. But if the doll is to be a baby or a small child,
the head must be much larger. The illustration shows
clearly what we mean. Notice that the two figures are the
same in height, yet one looks tall, the other short. The
baby doll's head is about one-fourth of its height; the man
doll's head about one-sixth or even less.

FACES. In making the doll's face look young or old
the features are differently placed on the head. And right
here let us point out one important thing about drawing
faces. Practically every amateur makes the mistake of drawing the eyes too high up on the face. Even if you draw cute,
childish features but place them too high, the face will
not look childish but will have an old look.

When drawing faces try placing the *eyes at the center
of the face* and see how much younger the face looks. Notice our two face illustrations—the child's eyes are placed
at the center of the head, the man's eyes above the center.

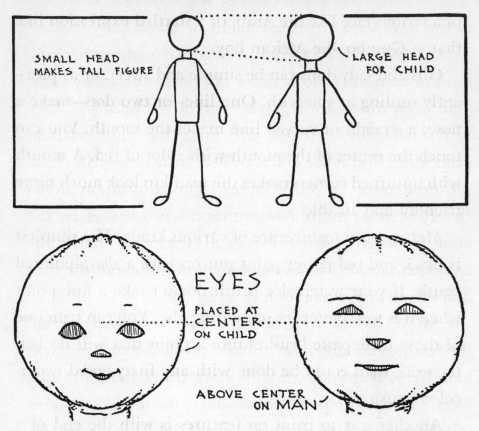

SMALL HEAD
MAKES TALL FIGURE

LARGE HEAD
FOR CHILD

EYES

PLACED AT
CENTER
ON CHILD

ABOVE CENTER
ON MAN

Usually we put in pins for the eyes until we get them properly placed. When the pins are removed their small holes serve as a guide for the painting.

There is very little to the drawing of faces—you can see that by the doll faces in the book. Any boy or man doll can have a jolly face like the Eskimo boy we call Nik-Nak, or a serious face like the Arab, or a startled expression like that of Gumbo, the African boy.

Girl and lady dolls can be simple and sweet, or as pleasantly smiling as you wish. One line—or two dots—make a nose; a straight or curved line makes the mouth. You can touch the center of the mouth with a dot of red. A mouth with upturned corners makes the manikin look much more friendly and likable.

Materials for features are of various kinds. The simplest is black and red poster paint put on with a *sharp*-pointed brush. If your watercolor brush doesn't take a fine point when it is wet, better try something else. You can trim one of those little paste brushes into a point that will do better work than could be done with any fuzzy-nosed watercolor brush.

Another way to paint on features is with the end of a matchstick. Dip it in poster color and when you paint it on, give the stick a little turn, to make the painted dot round. You can make these round dots for eyes, nose, and mouth.

Other ways to make features are: beads or embroidery knots for eyes; pen-and-ink features; eyebrow pencil for eyes and nose, rouge for mouth.

A warning! On some silk stocking material painted colors will spread; so test your paint (or ink) on the material before starting to paint the face. If it doesn't work well, you can make the features with stitches instead of paint.

In some of our drawings where we show a side view of the face, you may have noticed the merest suggestion of a nose and sometimes a sort of chin. Yet all the time you know perfectly well (if you've made a manikin) that noses and chins don't just push out by themselves on a ball-shaped head.

Here's how it is done, there's no trick to it at all. After the doll is made and all in costume, we take a big, strong needle with which to reach inside the head and push the filling around where we want it—some of it toward the chin. Then, with the needle, we pull out the stocking into a little nose that's nothing more than a tiny bump. We then push forward, with the needle, some of the head stuffing to help back up the nose we have made. It isn't very permanent, of course, but it does very well for a time.

The heads are soft enough so that your fingers can press

and pinch them into shape, with the aid of a needle to move the inside filling to one place or another. If you are making many of these dolls, we suggest that you try stuffing the heads with kapok instead of cotton—it is much softer. A big box of it costs 10¢ at fancy-work counters.

MAKING THE MANIKIN STAND ALONE is easy. We show two bases on one page. The first base is a paper picnic saucer such as bakeries use in wrapping foods. The feet are held by two wires from underneath. Sometimes only one wire will be needed for each foot, with the wires well twisted together underneath.

The second illustrated base is the cover of a paper food box. We show how you can place two long pins from outside the raised edge of the box, in through the doll's feet. This is a quickly made base, but you can tie or wire the feet to it, as is done with the other base.

There are many other things that can be used as bases —oats box lids or the lids of any small boxes. A cigar box lid is very good but since holes must be drilled in it for the wires it isn't quite so easy as the others. Beaverboard and cardboard of all kinds will make good stages for these midget actors.

16

BASES

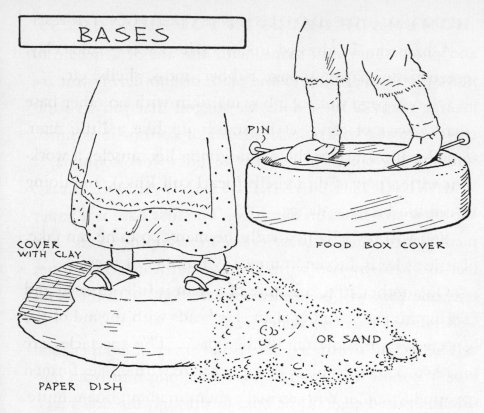

COVER
WITH CLAY

FOOD BOX COVER

PIN

PAPER DISH

OR SAND

6-INCH WIRE

SPECTACLES

BALD
SPOT

A base can be dressed up in various ways—sand, clay, green tissue paper, sponge rubber, moss, shells, etc.

On one page you see a boy manikin with no other base than a wad of clay, yet he stands up like a little man. Smaller illustrations show him giving his muscles a work-out with a pair of dumbbells (pearl cuff links), and doing a nimble bit of a dance.

You will be delighted with the many poses he can take. Little as he is, he can assume any number of them.

On another page this mite of a man is fully dressed and taking his ease in a big chair. He reads with the aid of the spectacles we show on another page. The spectacles are made of a six-inch piece of copper wire with circles formed around a pencil. You can make them in about one minute.

You may wonder how long a career one of these dolls may have. We tested the bare wire by bending it back and forth—not sharp bends but just about the way you would bend the doll in altering its pose. It took an average of fifty bends to break the wire, so you see these dolls have really strong constitutions. The copper wire for the making of one manikin costs a little over one cent.

HINTS. On our first dolls we made some mistakes that

HE CAN DO THINGS

CLAY

you need not make with yours. Our first—and worst—mistake was in winding the strips too loosely. Also, we tried to get along without doing any sewing at all. But after we bent our doll a few times the strips came loose and the doll was through doing tricks for us.

At first we did not make the separate coverings for hands and feet, so they came loose. But now that we sew coverings over the wire loops there is something to sew the winding strips onto, to anchor them securely.

In stuffing the stocking bodies you soon find that some kinds of stocking material stretch a great deal more than others. With such material a narrower piece should be used so the head won't be too large when stuffed.

When the head is too large you can always manage to nip it in. You can run a small pleat down the back seam and this will be concealed by the wig. You can also run a gathering thread around the neck part and draw the head in a bit there.

Then, *if the neck is too long,* a few stitches will pull the head down closer to the shoulders and shorten the neck. We often have to correct head sizes this way when the stocking has stretched more than we expected. It's not as troublesome as it sounds.

If the face goes wrong you can always cover the whole head with a little bag of stocking.

If anything goes wrong with the body, don't discard the doll. Just wrap it with cotton into a roly-poly shape and you will have a jolly Mr. Snowman, in town for the Christmas holidays.

MORE HINTS. The careful fastening of all ends will repay you for the small effort it takes. Anyone would rather take a few needless stitches than have part of a performing doll unroll itself after a few acrobatics. We know this can happen because it *did* happen.

The first time you make a doll its wrappings are likely to look a bit rough and bunchy. So to start with you might choose one whose clothing will cover it completely, like the little Eskimo or the Japanese or the Arab.

On your first doll avoid too much padding of the body and limbs—it will be easier to get the clothing on and off. Once you get the hang of it you can go ahead in your own way.

Then you will find it interesting to see how you can wind the strips thicker here and there so they give shape to the figure. Arms and legs can be given form, shoulders built out, and you can put knobby knees on such figures as Angus, the Scotch boy.

There are dozens of new tricks to try out and you will make some of the nicest discoveries! That's why this kind of doll-making is so much fun—smart new ideas keep popping into your head as you work.

PATTERNS have been kept as simple as possible so that the youngest of doll dressmakers can cut and sew the costumes. You will be charmed with the soft little patterns you can cut from Kleenex and with the way they may be fitted on the dolls. The handiest way to use the Kleenex patterns is in the doubled sheet as it comes from the box.

In our costume-making we left practically all edges raw, but here is a good chance for all the fine, careful needlework you wish to put into it.

MATERIALS FOR COSTUMES. The costuming of foreign dolls provides happy uses for the scrap bag. Go on a treasure hunt for bits of soft materials of every description and in every color.

Quaint little printed patterns are a prize find and so are batistes and dimities, chiffons and net, very soft silks and woolens. Tiny nosegay patterns and small designs of all kinds, along with stripes and checks and plain goods in gay colors—you can make use of them all.

Nicest to work with, perhaps, are thin old materials that have had the life washed out of them. Old handkerchiefs and nightdresses are examples—these will be treasure indeed!

There are plenty of materials for the taking, no matter where you live or how few materials there seem to be. In every home there are old stockings, gloves, and handkerchiefs, cast-off underwear and clothing, scraps of cloth, ribbon, lace, string, yarn, and probably some beads.

From these things a clever needle and snipping scissors can coax forth outfits quite elegant enough for princess or king, for prince or pauper—and just right for our little people.

You can do wonders with old gloves! From glove fingers you can make sleeves, trousers, and animal leg coverings. (See Nik-Nak and Bingo.) Glove fingertips make doll shoes and mittens, and smooth noses for animals like Bingo-the-burro and Chico-the-lamb.

Kid gloves make little leather coats and cunning saddles,

bridles, and harness. Silk gloves make wigs, doll stockings, and underwear. And all these are only a few of the things that gloves can make. The only gloves that one cannot use to advantage are the heavy ones and the string knits.

Stockings can be turned into tiny garments that drape into soft folds. Striped socks make little sweaters and caps, as well as blankets, ponchos, rugs, and cushions. The elastic cuffs of striped socks become ready-made skirts and petticoats.

Pieces of suède and chamois may come in handy. We made a fine Eskimo coat out of the ragged remnant of a window chamois. Other materials to save are fur scraps, felt, lace, net, feathers, beads, tiny buttons, little lingerie buckles, and glass-headed pins of every color. Uses can be found for colored twine and fancy cord, yarn, odds and ends of embroidery threads, scraps of ribbon, and such trifles.

SETTINGS

A ROSE-BOWERED doorway makes a good setting for some of the manikins. In the illustration we used it for a Dutch girl. It is made of a three-pound candy box and its cover. First, draw green lattice lines on the outside and inside of the box, on three sides. Cut a doorway in the bottom of the box. Then stand the box on end and place the cover over the back. This is so you can't see all the way through the doorway when the door is open but only into a shadowy place. Next, make a wide doorstep or porch out of a small box lid. Attach it with a little paste.

The vines are green string, wet with paste and dipped into tiny green paper scraps to look like leaves. Paste cut paper flowers here and there along the lattice, letting some of them hang over the edges a bit.

Open the door a little and set one of your dolls on the

CANDY BOX
AND COVER

BLOCK

DRAW LATTICE

doorstep where she can view the sights.

The next picture shows suggestions for making several kinds of trees for your settings.

One is an easily made paper tree. Cut a strip of green paper leaves with a good-sized piece of the paper left below them. Roll up this lower part into a tube, spreading the leaves out as you go along. Paste the tube, and slit its lower edge into tabs. These tabs can be pasted on a green paper or cardboard base.

Real evergreen twigs and sprays make a good-looking tropical tree. (See illustration.) Make a big loop at the bottom of the wire so the tree will stand. Bend a little loop or hook at the top end to help hold the sprays in place. Bind the twigs on, then cover the wire with tan-color wrappings of paper, crepe paper, stocking, or cloth.

Green sponge rubber can be snipped here and there until it takes on the form of a nice, fat little shrub. You can add more bits of rubber to it by using rubber cement for the pasting. A nail pushed up through a piece of cardboard goes on into the sponge rubber and makes a firm base.

Any little house looks better if it has a row of pine cone

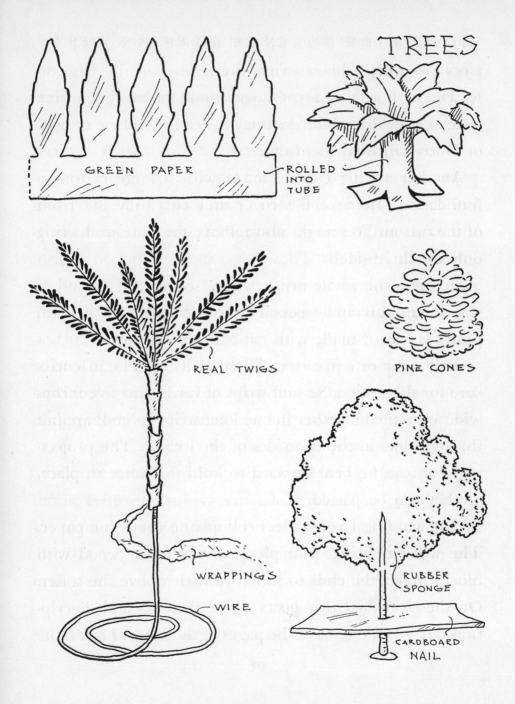

TREES

GREEN PAPER

ROLLED INTO TUBE

REAL TWIGS

PINE CONES

WRAPPINGS

WIRE

RUBBER SPONGE

CARDBOARD

NAIL

trees around it. These can be cemented to the base on which the house stands. Or you could put a single pine cone at each side of the doorway instead. Airplane cement or Duco will hold them there.

Another setting can be made with a large carton as foundation. Remove the cover and cut away the front of the carton. You might also remove the bottom, leaving only the three sides.

Decorate the whole inside with a scenic background of sky, mountains and trees. This can be painted in with poster colors or made with cut-out paper forms.

A circular or square cardboard fence makes an enclosure for the setting. Several strips of cardboard five inches wide are joined together in one long strip. Its ends are put through slots in the two sides of the carton. The projecting ends can be bent forward to hold the fence in place, or they can be pasted.

Our winding river is clear cellophane over blue paper. The wooden bridge is a piece of berry box wood with blocks under the ends to raise it a little above the water. On the river float tiny boats whose pictures and descriptions are given on one of the pages of the book, *The Home*

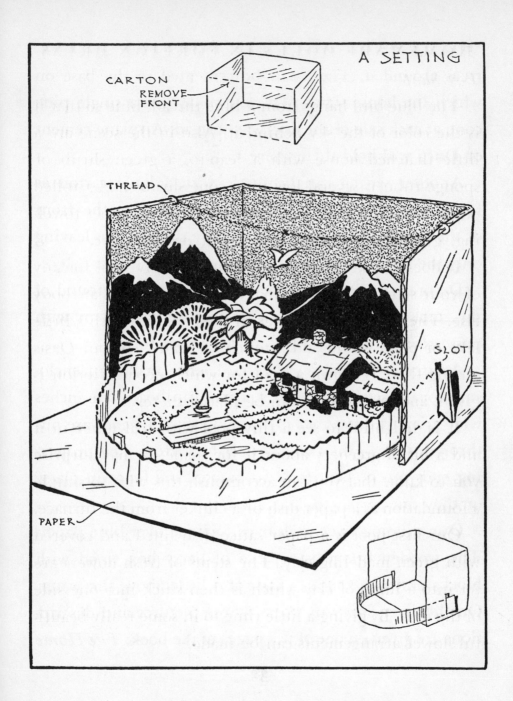

Toy Shop.

The blue bird hangs from a blue thread, blue so that it is the color of the sky behind it. Also in the scene are a little thatched house with a lean-to, a green shrub of sponge rubber, several low pine cone shrubs and a rolled paper tree. The grass may be made of green paper toweling, green-dyed sawdust, green felt or cloth, etc.

It doesn't take an artist to create a lovely pool for any of your settings. You can make one—and so can anybody else. There are many settings in the book in which a little lake or pond would add a touch of beauty. In our Oasis setting there is shown a pool for which no description is given, and one of these can be placed there.

It is delightful to see a tiny pool with real water in it and a bit of greenery about it for shade. It may surprise you to know that you can accomplish this with so simple a foundation as a paper dish or a clinker from the furnace.

Our first pool is a paper sauce dish lined and covered with green modeling clay. The stems of fresh flowers are set into a lump of clay which is then stuck into one side of the dish. By giving a little time to it, some really beautiful flower arrangements can be made.

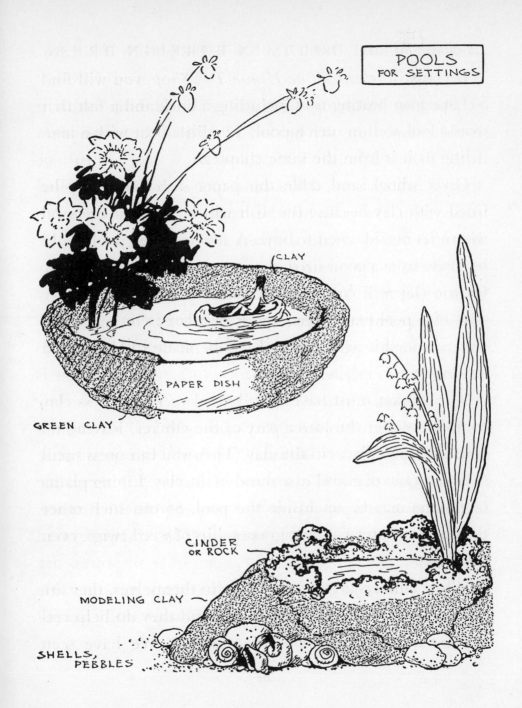

CLAY

PAPER DISH

GREEN CLAY

CINDER
OR ROCK

MODELING CLAY

SHELLS,
PEBBLES

If you will refer to *The Home Toy Shop,* you will find a chapter on floating toys including a duck and a fish that would look well in such a pool. The little boat with a man riding in it is from the same chapter.

On a school sand table the paper dish need only be lined with clay because the dish will be sunk in the sand where its outside won't show. A much larger pool could be made from a good-sized glass bowl—even a cracked one, for the clay will cover it and make it tight.

A nice pool may be made out of a large clinker! With water in it, this ugly material can be made to look like a mountain spring among rocks.

The clinker must have a hollow place in it. Press clay completely over the lower part of the clinker, leaving no cracks or open places in the clay. Then you can press small shells and bits of gravel in around in the clay. Living plants or flowers may be set inside the pool. So can such other things as evergreen sprays, grasses, bits of weed twigs, even just leaves.

While clinkers are not attractive in themselves, they are usually light in weight, easy to get, and they do help create a natural-looking spot in a setting. We have seen beautiful little rock gardens made from them by a florist.

There is still another way to make a tiny pool—the quickest and easiest way of all. It is nothing but a hollowed-out lump of green clay, yet it will hold water and never a drop will leak through. If there's any quicker way of making a real pool we'd like to hear about it!

On another page there is a plant whose pot is hidden under a steep bank of stones, pebbles, and moss. Before we forget it ourselves, let us remind you that here, among the stones, is a perfect place for any of those comical little cactus plants that may be sunning themselves in one of your windows.

If the tall potted plant were a pepper plant, or a jar of bitter-sweet, or some plant with berries on, it would make a setting by itself, that is, with one of your dolls beside it.

The doll could hold a basket on his arm while he reached for the apples—or whatever he thought they were. (There is a drawing of this basket in the Mexican chapter.)

When we mention the use of moss in a setting we refer to the grayish kind that florists use to put around plants. While it is not especially pretty, its value is that it aids the look of naturalness in a setting, and this is always an

35

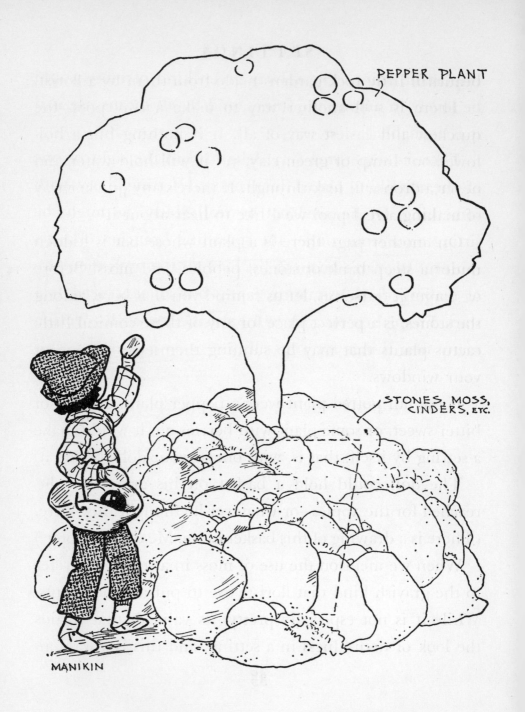

PEPPER PLANT

STONES, MOSS,
CINDERS, ETC.

MANIKIN

important point. The velvety green kind of moss would be lovely in among the stones, and by all means use it if it is available.

There is something very delightful in the sight of one of the manikins placed in a natural setting, busy with something. Or he need not be really busy; he might be sitting on a stone under the spreading branches of a geranium. We can't begin to list here all the ways there are of making these miniature lakes, but all you need is a start. From then on, you will have the joy of discovering many new things for yourself.

ESKIMO AND IGLOO

THIS is our little Eskimo, Nik-Nak. His body covering is dark tan stocking and his features are painted.

Although Nik-Nak isn't really dressed in furs at all, we can easily make him look as though he were. Real fur would be too bulky for the little fellow. Besides, furs are very hard to sew.

Notice the little mittens and shoes. They are the finger tips of old gloves. The shoes (or *mukluks*) are tan suède glove, bound around his ankles. The mittens are white. A few stitches across the wrists will give them shape and help keep them on.

Eskimos dress alike, that is, the men, women, and children wear the same style of clothing. There is the parka, which is a coat with hood attached. And the pants. They sometimes have shoes sewed to them just like a baby's

NIK-NAK
THE ESKIMO

GLOVE

GLOVE
FINGER

sleeping suit.

In summer the Eskimo wears only one fur suit. But in winter he puts another one on over it. His clothes make him look clumsy, but he isn't. All the real Eskimo clothes we have seen were made of such smooth skins as reindeer hide. The hood has a fluffy fur edging around the face to protect the eyes from whirling snow.

On the coat there is soft fur trimming around the hem and at the wrists. This is usually brownish wolverine fur. Coats are about knee length. Most of these reindeer coats are almost white, with splotches of tan here and there, much like calfskin.

We did not connect the coat and hood of Nik-Nak's suit. It would be too hard to get him into his clothes—or out of them. The top edge of the coat can be fitted neatly over the lower edges of the hood.

The hood has a seam down the back and some kind of fuzzy edging around the face. The slits make it possible to fit it in around the neck.

For a belt, use brown cord, a crocheted string, or something like that.

The coat illustrated was made from a pair of white fab-

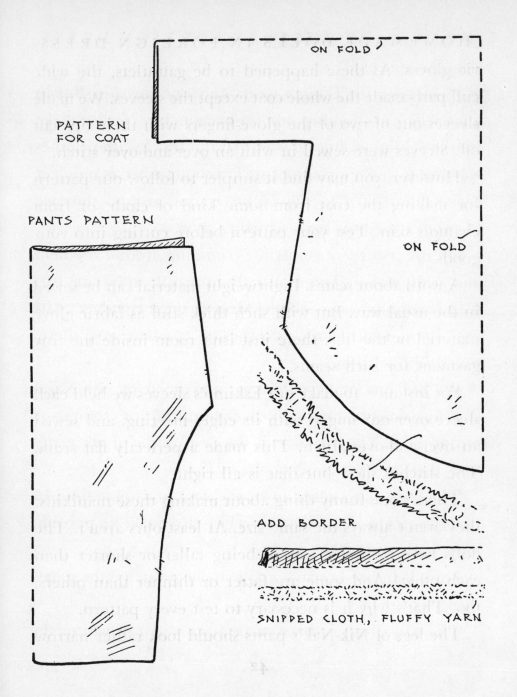

ON FOLD

PATTERN
FOR COAT

PANTS PATTERN

ON FOLD

ADD BORDER

SNIPPED CLOTH, FLUFFY YARN

ric gloves. As these happened to be gauntlets, the wide cuff parts made the whole coat except the sleeves. We made sleeves out of two of the glove-fingers with their tips cut off. Sleeves were sewed in with an over-and-over stitch.

However, you may find it simpler to follow our pattern for making the coat from some kind of cloth, or from chamois skin. Test your pattern before cutting into your goods.

A word about seams. Lightweight material can be sewed in the usual way. But with such thick stuff as fabric glove material or the like, there just isn't room inside the tiny garment for such seams.

For instance, to make our Eskimo's sleeves we held each sleeve over our finger, with its edges meeting, and sewed an over-and-over stitch. This made a perfectly flat seam. The stitches show but that is all right.

There's one funny thing about making these manikins; they aren't always the same size. At least ours aren't. The dolls have a strange way of being taller or shorter than each other! And some are fatter or thinner than others, too. That's why it is necessary to test every pattern.

The legs of Nik-Nak's pants should look rather narrow

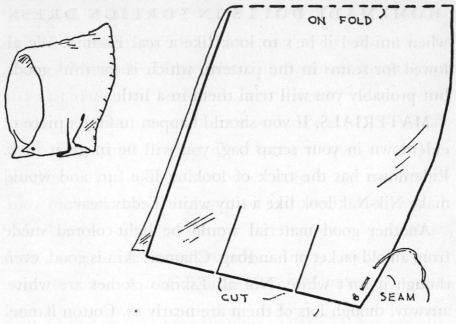

ON FOLD

CUT

SEAM

PATTERN FOR HOOD

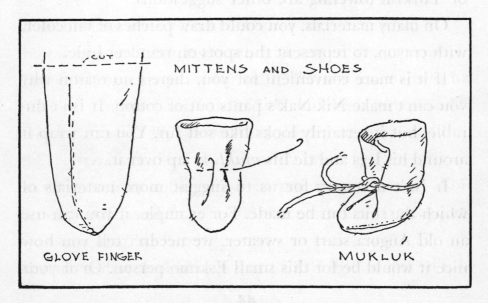

CUT

MITTENS AND SHOES

GLOVE FINGER

MUKLUK

when finished if he's to look like a real Eskimo. We allowed for seams in the pattern, which is for thin goods, but probably you will trim them in a little.

MATERIALS. If you should happen to find a piece of eiderdown in your scrap bag, you will be in great luck. Eiderdown has the trick of looking like fur, and would make Nik-Nak look like a tiny white Teddy bear.

Another good material would be light-colored suède from an old jacket or handbag. Chamois skin is good, even though it isn't white. Not all Eskimo clothes are white, anyway, though lots of them are nearly so. Cotton flannel or Turkish toweling are other suggestions.

On many materials, you could draw patches of tan color, with crayon, to represent the spots on reindeer hide.

If it is more convenient for you, there's no reason why you can't make Nik-Nak's pants out of cotton. It isn't durable, but it certainly looks like soft fur. You can wrap it around his legs and tie his *mukluks* up over it.

It isn't necessary for us to suggest more materials of which the suits can be made. For example, if you can use an old Angora scarf or sweater, we needn't tell you how nice it would be for this small Eskimo person. Or if your scrap bag contains soft woolens in any of the furry colors, you will certainly know what to do with them. Woolen socks and stockings are good, too.

Since an Eskimo must "catch" his own clothes, he has become very clever at using the few materials he finds around him in that frozen world. His materials consist of fish, animals, and snow! Yet of these he can provide his own food and clothing, his home, light, and all his needs for traveling on land and water.

His food is raw fish and meat. That's how he got the name "Eskimo," which means "eater of raw flesh."

His clothes are animal skins. He makes a fine boat from bones and skins. And he can build his house out of snow blocks and light it with seal fat.

SETTING. We arranged the setting in the lid of a large hat box. There is a poster background fastened inside the back of the lid. The poster had to have something behind it to keep it upright.

The poster mountains are a dull, soft blue. The deep blue sky has snow flurries painted on it. These blues in the background set off the whiteness of snow as no other color can do. Blue makes white look cold—and clean! Instead of snowflakes, you could paint in the Aurora Bore-alis and get some real color into the scene.

Igloo. Everyone knows that Eskimos don't always live in snow igloos. But other kinds of Eskimo houses aren't nearly so attractive. So we have made an igloo in the quick-est, easiest way possible.

It is an upturned mixing bowl, covered with cotton tied with thread. The white thread was tied around the cotton-covered bowl just as you tie a package. It crossed under-neath and on top, first in quarters, then in eighths. A few round-and-round threads were added to the sides. This outlines the snow blocks.

The tunnel was wrapped the same way. It was made from a kitchen cleanser box. When the ends are cut off and a little of its side cut away, you have an arched card-board just the shape of a tunnel.

An Eskimo setting is very easy to make. The quick way to represent snow is with cotton, of course. Torn cotton can be spread about to look like soft snow. There's no need to use expensive hospital cotton when you can get a big ten-cent roll at the dime-store embroidery counter. Un-fold this roll of cotton into a thin sheet about 40 by 50

POSTER

BOX LID

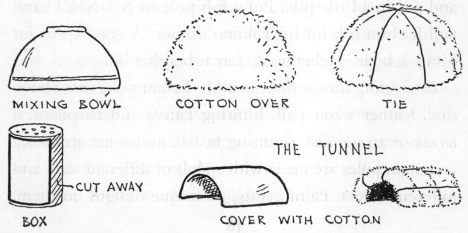

MIXING BOWL   COTTON OVER   TIE

BOX

CUT AWAY

THE TUNNEL

COVER WITH COTTON

inches. Tear off a long strip, double it, and cover the igloo and tunnel.

This leaves a single sheet of the cotton about a yard square. Part of this makes the snowy ground for the setting.

If you want to make footprints in the snow, snip loose some small tufts of cotton but don't take them out—leave them there. The cut-away part looks like the kick-ups of snow that our feet make.

The *fishing hole* was made by cutting a small jagged hole in the cotton and putting a piece of black paper beneath it.

Something else you can do is to lay chips of "ice" beside the hole as though Nik-Nak had just chopped the hole. "Ice" will be wrinkled-up cellophane cut into small bits and put in a little pile. Put a fish pole in Nik-Nak's hand and let him fish for his Eskimo dinner. A good spear for him is a bone crochet hook. Lay it beside him.

Interesting things you can add: Totem pole, snowshoes, sled, leather water pail, hunting lances and harpoons, a *kayak* or an *oomiak* (hunting boats), and some animals.

Totem poles are made with spools of different sizes and different colors. Paint gaudy, grotesque designs on them.

The bottom spool should be glued to a base of cardboard. A piece of balloon stick is set into the bottom spool; the other spools are impaled on it.

The animals could be a Husky dog, polar bear, seal, or reindeer. All would be made about as described in the Mexican chapter. We do not illustrate any of these animals but you can easily find pictures of them as a help in getting them to look right.

MEXICAN PEDRO GOES TO MARKET

PEDRO is a Mexican boy doll. His skin is made of brown stocking. His black stocking hair is made as described in the first chapter.

Pedro's shirt and trousers are white. An old, soft handkerchief would be good material for making them.

As you see in the small picture, the shirt is cut double, with the fold at the top. The easiest way to make it is to draw lines where the two side seams are to be, and sew these seams before cutting away the goods under the arms. Last, we cut the front opening of the shirt, and slit the neck part just a trifle at the sides.

The trousers are made with a fold at one side, a seam at the other. Then we sew the two inner leg seams (about one-quarter inch apart) and cut between them. These stitches should be close and firm.

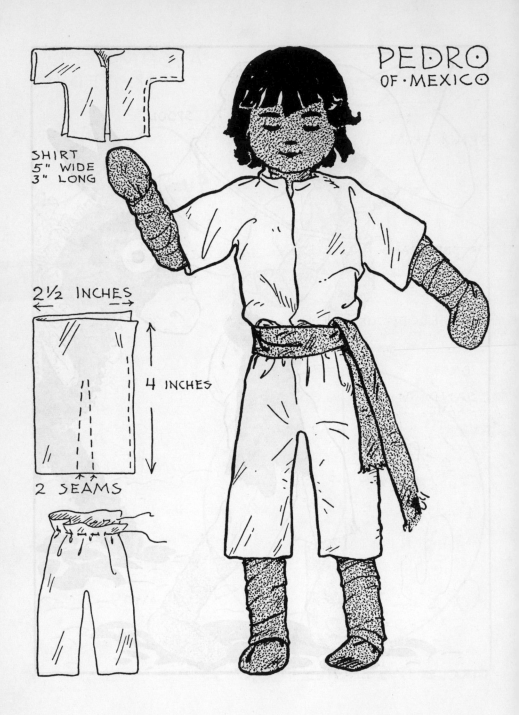

SHIRT
5" WIDE
3" LONG

2½ INCHES

4 INCHES

2 SEAMS

PEDRO
OF·MEXICO

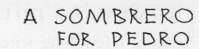

A SOMBRERO
FOR PEDRO

BEND BRIM UPWARD

JOIN EDGES OF CROWN

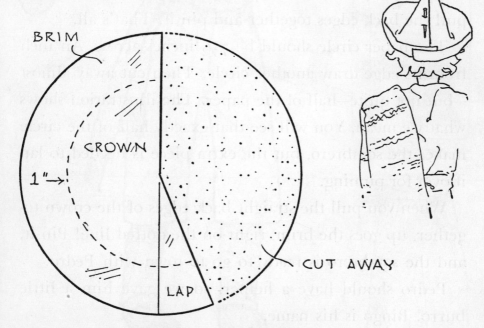

BRIM

1"→

CROWN

LAP

CUT AWAY

CIRCLE 7½ INCHES ACROSS

Run a few long stitches around the waistline of the trousers for a gathering string.

Pedro's sash gives a colorful touch to his costume. We had a shred of soft orange-color silk, so that's what we made our sash of. Any gaily colored scrap of silk, cotton, or ribbon will do, if it isn't too heavy or stiff. The thinner it is, the better.

Making the sombrero for Pedro is even simpler than it sounds. The materials are a circle of paper and a pin. Cut out the circle, bend up the brim a little all around, pull the back edges together and pin it. That's all.

The paper circle should be 7½ inches across. An inch from its edge draw another circle. Then cut away almost —but not quite—half of the paper. The illustration shows what we mean. You will see that exactly half of the circle makes the sombrero, but the extra piece is needed to lap it over for pinning.

When you pull the straight back edges of the crown together, up goes the brim, right on the dotted line! Pin it, and the sombrero is ready to go to town with Pedro.

Pedro should have a helper, so we gave him a little burro. Bingo is his name.

A BURRO — BINGO IS HIS NAME

He was made of corrugated board and wire, padded out a little and wrapped with strips of cotton sock. We then dressed Bingo in a fuzzy gray wool glove.

Bingo's eyes are cloth reinforcements, his white nose a glove finger, and he wears his tail in a braid.

This little burro stands up firmly on his stout woolly legs. And that's not all—he can carry Pedro on his back!

You can bend Bingo's head and legs in almost any direction and they will stay where you put them. He can even be made to sit down on his hind legs and balk!

You will notice one picture of him with a big bundle of twigs tied on his back.

Now let's get to work on him. To begin with, cut a piece of flexible corrugated board 3 inches wide, 12 inches long. Roll it up tightly and tie it. The roll will be about 2 inches across.

Next, cut 3 pieces of wire, each 18 inches long. One will make the head and neck. The other two will be the legs. Double each of the leg wires, and push it through holes in the corrugated roll. These holes should be about one-half inch in from the ends of the roll. Punch the holes with a nut pick or the like. Don't try to make them with the

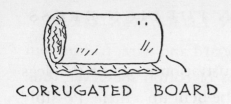

CORRUGATED BOARD

HOW TO MAKE
THE BURRO

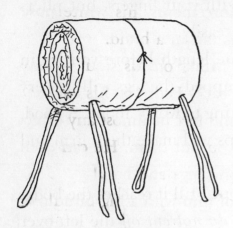

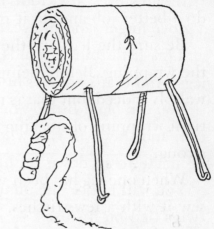

PUSH LEG-WIRES
THROUGH HOLES AND WRAP WITH STRIPS

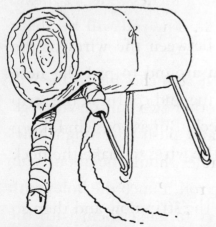

CARRY STRIP ACROSS

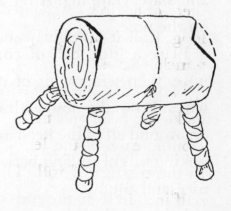

TRIM A LITTLE AT
CENTER OF TOP

wire itself.

As you can see from the illustrations, two of the legs will have raw ends which must be bent up a little. Possibly you could bend these points with your fingers, but pliers do a better job and do it more easily.

Be sure the legs are the same length before you begin the wrapping. Before being wrapped, the legs will be very wabbly indeed, but that is nothing to worry about. A good, tight wrapping of stocking strips will make them firm and strong.

When one leg has been wrapped till it reaches the body, sew it with a few stitches, but *do not cut off* the left-over part of the strip. Instead, carry it across to the other leg and start wrapping. After all four legs are finished, begin on the nose.

Place a little ball of cotton between the wires of the nose, then wrap a bit of cotton around to pad the nose wires. Wrap the nose with stocking and continue the strip on around all of the head and neck. But as you wind, keep poking bits of stuffing between the wires to make the neck nice and plump.

It is a good plan to criss-cross the strip now and then so

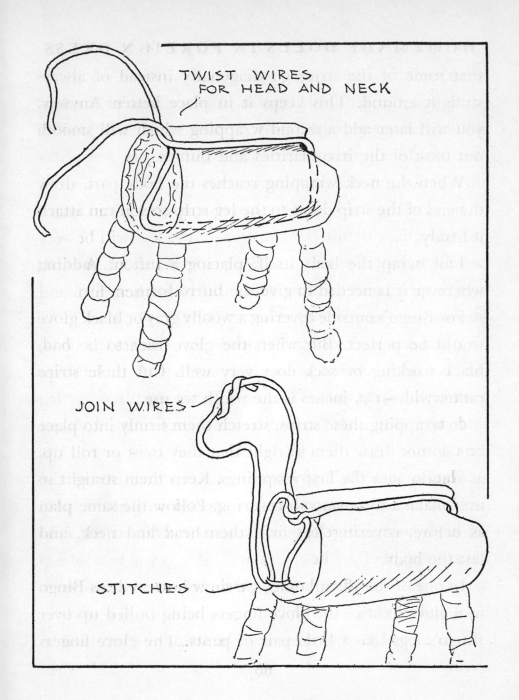

TWIST WIRES
FOR HEAD AND NECK

JOIN WIRES

STITCHES

that some of the strips go diagonally instead of always straight around. This keeps it in place better. Anyway, you will later add a second wrapping which will smooth out most of the irregularities and bumps.

When the neck wrapping reaches the body part, draw the end of the strip down to the leg strip so you can attach it firmly.

Last, wrap the body itself, placing a tuft of padding wherever it is needed to give the burro form.

For Bingo's outside covering a woolly gray or black glove would be perfect. But when the glove isn't to be had, black stocking or sock does very well. Cut these strips rather wide—1½ inches is the width we use.

In wrapping these strips, stretch them firmly into place but do not draw them so tight that they twist or roll up, as you do with the first wrappings. Keep them straight so they make a nice, smooth covering. Follow the same plan as before, covering legs first, then head and neck, and last the body.

In one of the illustrations, we show how to dress Bingo in a glove. Notice the glove fingers being pulled up over Bingo's legs like a little pair of pants. The glove fingers

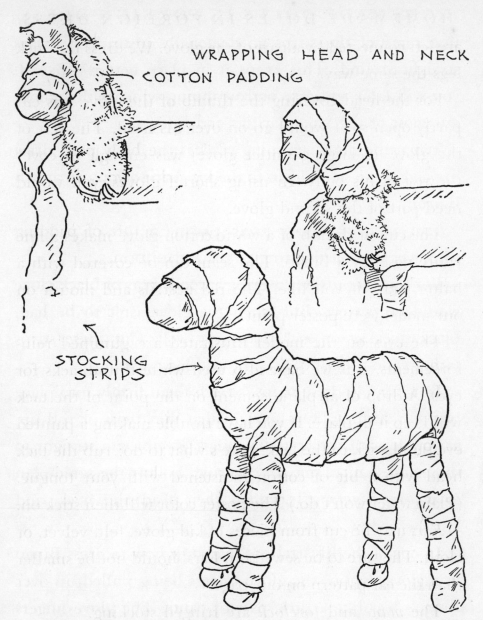

WRAPPING HEAD AND NECK

COTTON PADDING

STOCKING STRIPS

THE BURRO READY FOR AN OUTSIDE COAT

are left connected by a part of the glove. We dress the back legs the same way.

For the head covering the thumb of the glove was cut partly open so it would go on over his head. The rest of the glove (a large gauntlet glove) was enough to cover the rest of his body. In using shorter gloves, you would need part of the second glove.

The cut-off thumb of a white cotton glove makes a fine white nose for a burro. The seam can be covered with a halter strap, if you like. The red nostrils and mouth on our model were poster paint.

The *eyes* on the model illustrated are gummed reinforcements. But we have also used white thumbtacks for eyes. A drop of airplane cement on the point of the tack will keep it in place. If you have trouble making a painted eye-pupil stick to the tack, here's what to do: rub the tack head with a bit of cotton moistened with your tongue. (Plain water won't do.) The poster color will then stick on.

Ears may be cut from pieces of kid glove, felt, velvet, or cloth. They are to be sewed on. Ears should not be smaller than the ear pattern on our page.

The *mane* and *forelock* are fringed stocking.

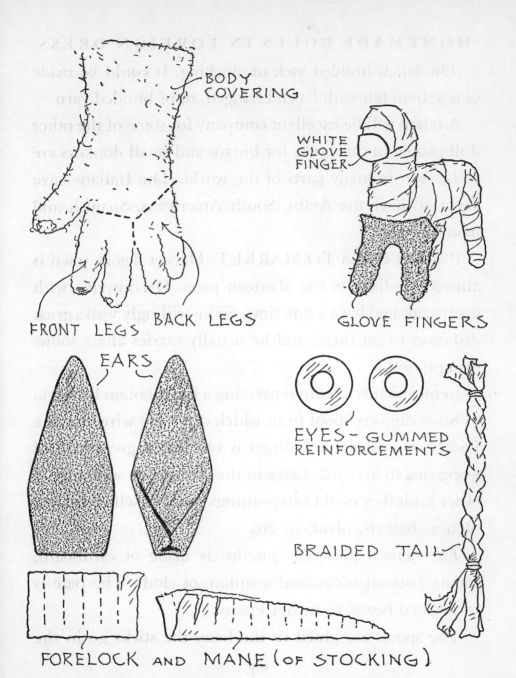

BODY
COVERING

WHITE
GLOVE
FINGER

FRONT LEGS   BACK LEGS   GLOVE FINGERS

EARS

EYES - GUMMED
REINFORCEMENTS

BRAIDED TAIL

FORELOCK and MANE (OF STOCKING)

The *tail* is braided sock or stocking. It could be made of a strip of felt with its end fringed, or of braided yarn.

A burro will be excellent company for some of the other doll-people in this book, for burros and small donkeys are to be seen in many parts of the world. The Italians have them, so have the Arabs, South Americans, Spanish and many others.

PEDRO GOES TO MARKET. Market day in town is almost a holiday to the Mexican peon. He can visit with his friends and have a fine time. So he willingly walks great distances to get there, and he usually carries along something to sell.

In one picture, Pedro is carrying a big spool on his back. (This is the very spool from which came the wire to make Pedro's own skeleton.) Bingo is carrying a great load of wood tied to his back. Later in the chapter we will suggest other loads they might carry—things you yourself can make, such as baskets, blankets, etc.

The market place (or *puesto*) is made of cardboard, spools, balloon sticks, and a square of cloth. The base is corrugated board 12 inches square.

The spools are glued to the base, the sticks go in the

A MARKET

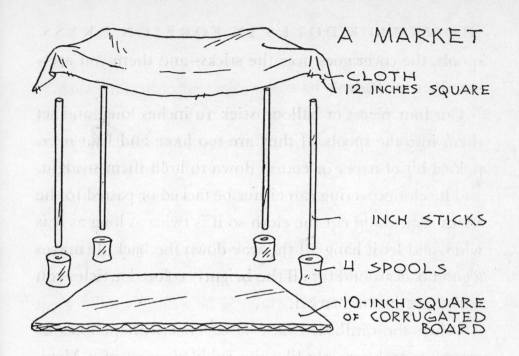

CLOTH
12 INCHES SQUARE

INCH STICKS

4 SPOOLS

10-INCH SQUARE
OF CORRUGATED
BOARD

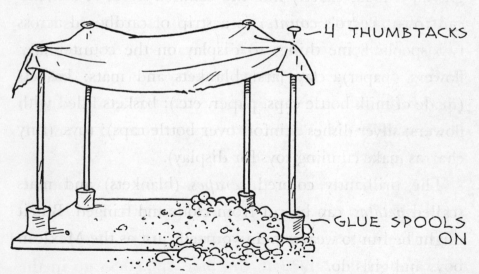

4 THUMBTACKS

GLUE SPOOLS
ON

GRAVEL 'PAVING' HIDES BASE

spools, the cover goes over the sticks—and there you are—a market for Pedro!

Cut four pieces of balloon stick 10 inches long, and set them into the spools. If they are too loose and lean over, poke a bit of paper or cotton down to hold them straight.

The cloth covering can either be tacked or pasted to the sticks. You could cut the cloth so it is twice as long as it is wide, and let it hang all the way down the back. It makes a good background for all the brightly colored articles you will place in the market.

When the cardboard base is covered with pebbles or gravel, it looks exactly like the cobbled street of a Mexican town. Pedro's *counter* is a strip of cardboard across two spools. Some things to display on the counter are: flowers (paper); clay jars; blankets and mats; baskets (made of milk bottle caps, paper, etc.); baskets filled with flowers; silver dishes (tinfoil over bottle caps); toys (tiny charms make cunning toys for display).

The brilliantly colored *serapes* (blankets) and mats (called *petates*) can be cut from cloth and fringed. But it might be fun to weave them yourself, just as the Mexican boys and girls do.

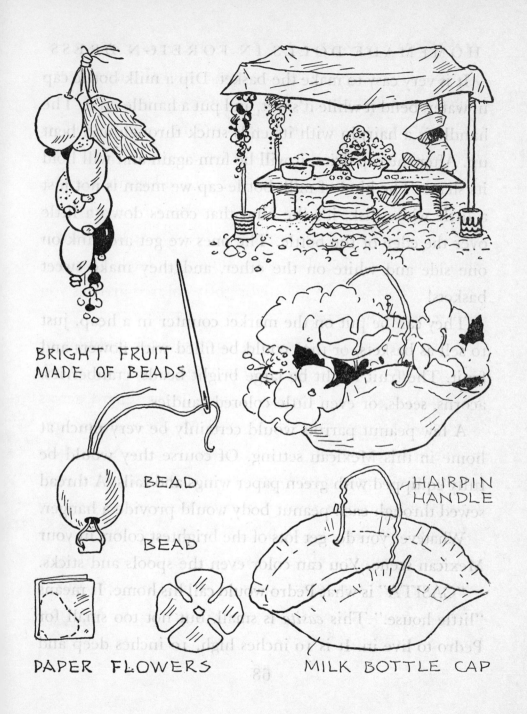

BRIGHT FRUIT
MADE OF BEADS

BEAD

BEAD

HAIRPIN
HANDLE

PAPER FLOWERS

MILK BOTTLE CAP

It is very easy to make the basket. Dip a milk bottle cap in water, bend it while it's wet, and put a handle on it. The handle is a hairpin with its ends stuck through and bent up. After the cap dries, it will be firm again and will hold its shape. The kind of milk bottle cap we mean is not just a little white disk, it's the kind that comes down a little over the edge of the bottle. The ones we get are pink on one side and white on the other, and they make sweet baskets!

They can be put on the market counter in a heap, just to sell as baskets, or they could be filled with flowers and fruit. The fruit might be large bright beads, cranberries, acorns, seeds, or even little colored candies.

A few peanut parrots would certainly be very much at home in this Mexican setting. Of course they would be fully equipped with green paper wings and tails. A thread sewed through each peanut body would provide a hanger.

Whatever you do, get lots of the brightest colors in your Mexican scene. You can color even the spools and sticks.

"CASITA" is what Pedro would call his home. It means "little house." This *casita* is small, but not too small for Pedro to live in. It is 10 inches high, 10 inches deep and

16 inches wide. Four shirt cardboards make the house walls, and corrugated board its tile roof.

This *casita* is supposed to be of adobe; that's why we made the door and window outlines rounded and uneven. The gray side of a shirt board is just about the right color for an adobe house.

Shirt boards do not take large areas of water color very well. But if you want color on the house walls, you could put it on in spatter work. Dip an old toothbrush into poster color and scrape it across a stick, while holding it over the cardboard. When doing spatter work, you need plenty of newspapers spread all about while the work is going on.

The two ends of the house are bent inward, as the illustration shows, for pasting them inside the other two walls. Instead of pasting, you can attach the walls with paper fasteners, if you wish.

The door and window are easiest to cut before the house is put together. Cut the door open along three sides only, leaving the fourth side attached as a hinge for bending the door inward. Do the same with the window.

Mexican houses do not have many windows, so one or

two will be enough. Small window panes are drawn on. Boards and hinges are drawn on the door. The door looks well when it is painted a handsome bright blue or some other cheerful color.

You probably know that the triangular piece of cardboard is the gable for the roof to rest on. It is 10 inches long, 4 inches high. This leaves a two-inch space for pasting it inside the house wall. The other two inches of it are cut to a point, as you see. Make two of these gables, one for each end of the house.

All ready, now, for the roof. Most homes in Mexico have low roofs with stubby eaves. Some of the roofs are thatched, but a tile roof is much easier for us to make, and besides, it can be painted a pleasant color.

We made this roof of corrugated board 12 by 18 inches. Then we cut it part way through at the ridge so it would bend. When you make the roof, be careful that you don't measure it with the ridges going the wrong way. It would look funny if the tiles went sideways instead of up and down!

We like pink tiles on a house so we painted our tiles with poster colors in vermilion and white, mixed together.

THE CASITA
(LITTLE HOUSE)

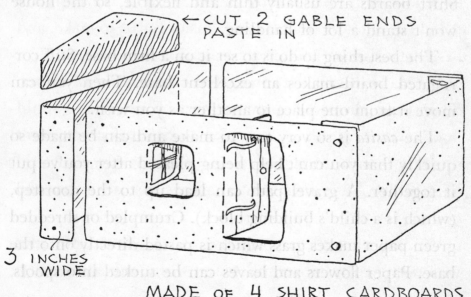

← CUT 2 GABLE ENDS
PASTE IN

3 INCHES
WIDE

MADE OF 4 SHIRT CARDBOARDS

It's lots easier to do this painting with an old toothbrush instead of a regular water-color brush. We did not paint into every speck of the hollows, either, but sketched across the ridges with color. This gives somewhat the effect of old, worn tiles.

To attach the roof, lay it in place, then turn the whole house upside down. The joining is done with gummed paper tape. Connect the ridge of the roof to the peak of the house, first at one end, then the other. Finish one half of the roof before starting the other.

You mustn't expect this *casita* to be a very strong house. Shirt boards are usually thin and flexible, so the house won't stand a lot of handling.

The best thing to do is to set it on a firm base. Stiff corrugated board makes an excellent base. Then you can move it from one place to another as you wish.

The *casita* is so very easy to make and can be made so quickly that you can't help being pleased after you've put it together. A gravel path can lead up to the doorstep, (which is a child's building block). Crumpled or shredded green paper makes grass which is pasted directly onto the base. Paper flowers and leaves can be tucked into spools, for plants. A tiny real cactus or two would look splendid standing near the house.

See those vines on the wall? They're green string, wet with paste and dipped into shreds of green paper. If you care to make a few palm trees for the garden, you will find them described in the chapter on Arab dolls.

It will be easy to think up other things you can add to make a real Mexican home for Pedro. For instance, a hood over the doorway. This would be a little piece of corrugated board pasted to the roof from underneath, over the doorway. It would be painted to match the roof.

And don't forget strings of peppers and gourds!

INDIAN MOTHER AND BABY

PALOMA is a Pueblo Indian mother. Her skin color is of a rather deep tan. Her body is sturdy and strong as are the bodies of all members of her tribe.

Paloma is wearing a white blouse and a sky-blue dress with a wide red belt. Always she wears curious little leather boots of milky white.

The skirt is softly gathered, then its folds are smoothed down so the skirt does not billow out too much.

No pattern is given here for the white blouse. There are plenty of blouse patterns in the book for you to choose from and you can cut out a Kleenex pattern to try on your lady. Begin with a piece about 7 inches wide and 6 inches deep. Allow a little fullness in the sleeves so they can be gathered at the wrists. The fold over Paloma's shoulder is blue like her skirt. It is a straight piece of goods wide

WHITE BLOUSE

BLUE DRESS
RED BELT

BRIGHT SHAWL

enough to go halfway around her waist and long enough to go under the belt at front and back. On our Indian model the piece measures 6 inches long, 3 inches wide. We trimmed it a little where it goes under her left arm. A bright red ribbon makes the stiff, wide belt. Its symbolic designs may be made either with paint or with threads, in white or colors.

The wig is a piece of soft, black silk sock. It is so cut that Paloma's hair, at the sides, will be on a level with her chin. That shorter left side of the wig—as the pattern appears on the page—is the edge that goes around her face. The large remaining portion of the wig is drawn smoothly to the back of her head, then tied with gay-colored yarn into an odd double twist of hair. You will notice what seems to be a part in Paloma's glossy black hair. A brown thread gives that appearance. Sewed through the head, it holds the wig on, and should be the color of her skin, for the best effect.

Paloma's blanket is a bright shawl. And here's your chance to use the most surprising of colors. Our shawl was the cut-out center of the brightest five-cent handkerchief we could find. (The left-over border will make a lot of

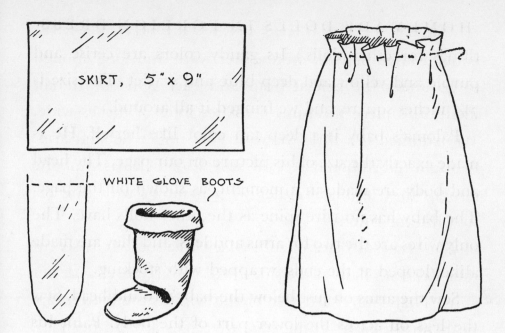

SKIRT, 5" x 9"

WHITE GLOVE BOOTS

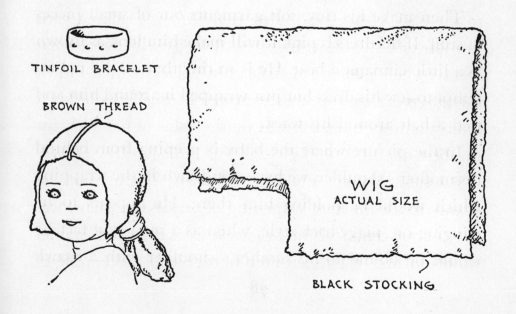

TINFOIL BRACELET

BROWN THREAD

WIG
ACTUAL SIZE

BLACK STOCKING

things for other dolls.) Its gaudy colors are cerise and purple and yellow and deep blue and scarlet. The size is 7½ inches square, and we fringed it all around.

Paloma's baby is a deep tan color like herself. He is made exactly the size of his picture on our page. The head and body are made in a moment, as shown on the page. The baby has no wire spine as the other dolls have. The only wires are the two for arms and legs, and they are made alike, looped at the ends, wrapped with stocking.

Sew the arms on just below the baby's round head. Sew the legs on across the lower part of the body. Paint his face and cut him a wig from the thumb of a black glove.

Then make his tiny, soft garments out of small pieces of stuff. If his dress is pink it will make him look as brown as a little cinnamon bear. He is so tiny that we did not attempt to sew his dress but just wrapped it around him and tied a belt around his waist.

In the picture where the baby is peeping from behind his mother's shoulder, we have not drawn in the wrapping which would be holding him there. He appears to be clinging on, piggy-back style, when as a matter of fact he would be bound to his mother's shoulder with a shawl.

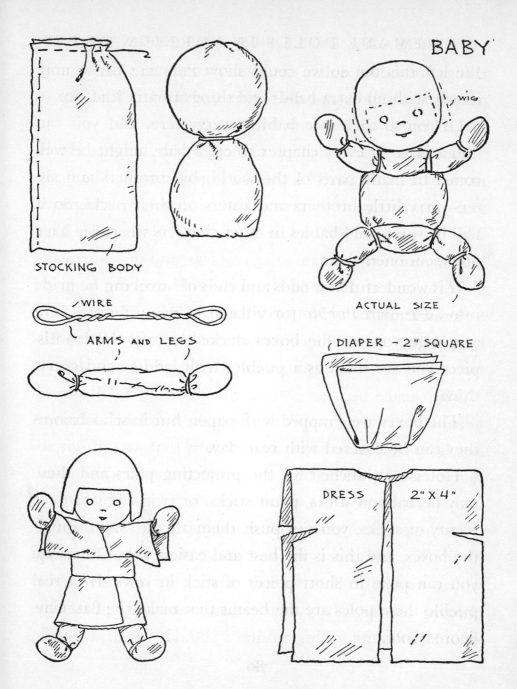

BABY

STOCKING BODY

WIRE

ARMS AND LEGS

WIG

ACTUAL SIZE

DIAPER – 2" SQUARE

DRESS   2" X 4"

We left this out so we could show Paloma's dress more clearly with no extra bands and things to mix it all up.

Of course there are babies everywhere, and you can find a place in every chapter where a baby might be welcome. In many parts of the world, big brothers and sisters carry little brothers and sisters on their backs. So it will be fun to add babies in other chapters where we have not mentioned them.

It is wonderful how odds and ends of boxes can be made into an Indian *Pueblo* (or village) of many terraces. On one page you see the boxes stacked up; in the frontispiece you see them as a pueblo, with ladders and everything.

The boxes are wrapped with paper, but in schoolrooms they can be covered with real clay.

Holes are punched for the projecting poles and these may be balloon sticks, plant sticks, or twigs. If you have plenty of sticks, you can push them all the way through the boxes, and this is the best and easiest way. Otherwise you can poke in short pieces of stick in rows. In a real pueblo these poles are the beams that make the flat, clay-floored roof.

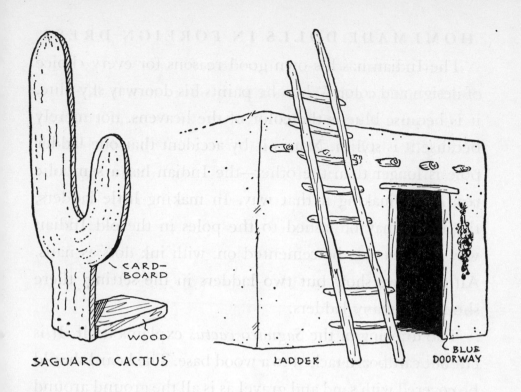

SAGUARO CACTUS

CARD-
BOARD

WOOD

LADDER

BLUE
DOORWAY

CARTONS AND BOXES FOR PUEBLO

The Indian has his own good reasons for every choice of design and color. When he paints his doorway sky-blue, it is because blue is the color of the heavens, not merely because it is stylish. Nor is it by accident that one ladder pole is longer than the other—the Indian has a symbolic reason for making it that way. In making little ladders, the rungs may be lashed to the poles in the old Indian way, or they may be cemented on, with ink dots as nails. Although we show but two ladders in the setting, there should be many ladders.

The drawing of the *Saguaro cactus* explains itself. It is cut-out cardboard tacked to a wood base. The board should be covered with sand and gravel as is all the ground around the pueblo.

Pole sun shelters are built by many Indian tribes, not the Pueblo Indians alone. But on the sun-drenched mesas where the pueblos are, pole shelters are really valuable. You could add one to the pueblo, making it of sticks and cardboard.

Strings of scarlet peppers beside the doorways add charming color accents. Make them of beads or whatever else you have handy.

In the frontispiece, Paloma is busily at work painting jars with her brush of yucca fiber. Her little bench is a cardboard box and its cover, covered with tan paper.

There are many excellent books about these interesting people, the Pueblo Indians. In them you can find pictures of pottery, baskets, jewelry, rugs and hangings, looms, ovens, and all manner of things that make up Pueblo Indian life. These and other things can be added to make the pueblo setting a fascinating and busy scene. A burro, like Bingo of Mexico, would be a good addition, too.

PANCHO OF PERU

PANCHO is a South American Indian who lives in an earth-floored adobe hut in Peru. The hut is so small that Pancho must stoop to enter the doorway. Since there is no window, the inside of the hut is dark as a pocket, but Pancho is a sheep-herder, so he is outdoors most of the time.

The covering of this figure is dark tan stocking. The wind-blown hair is a wig of stocking as black as coal. The eyes and nose are black ink drawn on with a brush. The mouth is red poster paint.

Pancho's shirt and white trousers are like those of Pedro from Mexico. The only difference is that the trousers are cut one inch wider and one inch longer.

A mended stocking-toe made the hat. Turn it up at the front, down in the back.

PANCHO

PONCHO
6 × 8

HAT

Pancho's most treasured garment is his wool poncho, and a clever affair it is, too. It becomes his overcoat when he puts his head through the opening in its center.

At night it's his bed blanket; in rainy weather, his slicker. And in between whiles, the poncho may be used as a saddle blanket on the back of a burro or a llama.

Pancho weaves his own poncho. Notice how simply it is made—an oblong with a slit in the center. No buttons, pins, or belt are needed.

In making a poncho for your own little South American, you can do as Pancho does. If he has materials for a striped one, fine! That's what he likes best. Otherwise he makes it of such plain dark wool as he may have.

A striped sock is about the quickest and easiest material of which to make it. Any striped goods or soft, old wool will make a good one. The advantage of knitted goods is that it can be stretched over the doll's head without having such a large opening cut in it as is needed for cloth. Washed material usually falls into softer folds than new material.

We made eight ponchos from one five-cent dishcloth that had stripes knitted into it. The dishcloth was double, so we cut it into single thicknesses. The size of the poncho is about 6 by 8 inches. Raveled edges give quite the proper finish.

HUT. Our hut is a close copy of a native Peruvian one. Though it was so very primitive, yet it had a pink tile roof.

We made our roof of corrugated board 12 inches wide, 8 inches deep from front to back. In the Mexican chapter you will find complete directions for attaching and painting this kind of roof.

The illustrated hut was made from a small, stiff carton in which a flatiron had been shipped. The carton was 9½ inches wide, 5 inches deep and 5½ inches high. When its cover flaps were opened out, the front was 8½ inches high. The two ends were an inch higher, so we cut them into a point, as you see.

We removed the bottom of the carton so it would be easier to attach the roof, and also so the hut could have a real dirt floor. The doorway is framed with "timbers," that is, with pieces of stick.

Before plastering the hut with gray modeling clay (for adobe) we placed several long sticks so they would project from under the eaves. To help hold them in place, notches were cut in the ends of the house. A few pieces of mending tape or adhesive tape of any kind make them secure.

If you plan to spread clay over the hut walls, use a firm carton. A friendly druggist or hardware man can probably be depended on to give you a suitable one. The size might be a little larger than ours, but not much.

SETTING. The ground around the hut is sand and gravel. It could be made of a number of other things—sawdust, clay, dirt, or even tan paper. A tree and a shrub or two add greatly to the attractiveness of a setting.

For the tree, a small real branch can bloom out with foliage of one kind or another—crumpled green paper, Easter grass, cut-paper leaves, etc. Even poster trees can be used.

Green sponge rubber makes nice, chubby-looking shrubs. Cut a small cardboard base, push a nail up through it and spear the piece of sponge on the nail point. A sprinkling of sand will conceal the base. Sea sponge can be used the same way if it is dyed green.

Many small things can be added to make this tiny homestead look lived-in. Stand a few bundles of long grasses against the house. Those will be sheaves of barley or

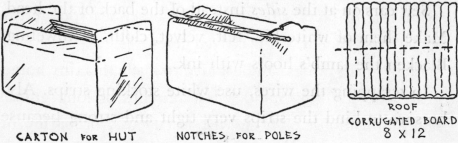

CARTON FOR HUT   NOTCHES FOR POLES   ROOF
CORRUGATED BOARD
8 X 12

grain. There can be a scattering of kindling wood near the house. A stone beside the doorway will be a place for Pancho to sit and think.

We stood a deep clay jar in the yard. That's for pounding cornmeal. At the front of the setting, Pancho is seen feeding Chico, his pet lamb, from a leather bottle (glove fingertip).

LAMB. Chico, the lamb, is white and woolly.

He is made in the same general way as the burro in the Mexican chapter, but you use different lengths of wire. Cut wires 8 inches long for the legs, 12 inches long for the head part. This allows one inch for twisting the wire ends together at the back of the neck.

When you bend the wires into a head shape make it no longer than an ordinary marble. After the lamb is padded and wrapped, pull a white glove fingertip up over the nose, and draw the eyes, nostrils, and mouth with ink.

Sew ears on at the *sides* instead of the back of the head. Make them of white kid, felt, velvet, cloth, or toweling. Blacken the lamb's hoofs with ink.

In wrapping the wires, use white stocking strips. Also be sure to bind the strips very tight and strong because

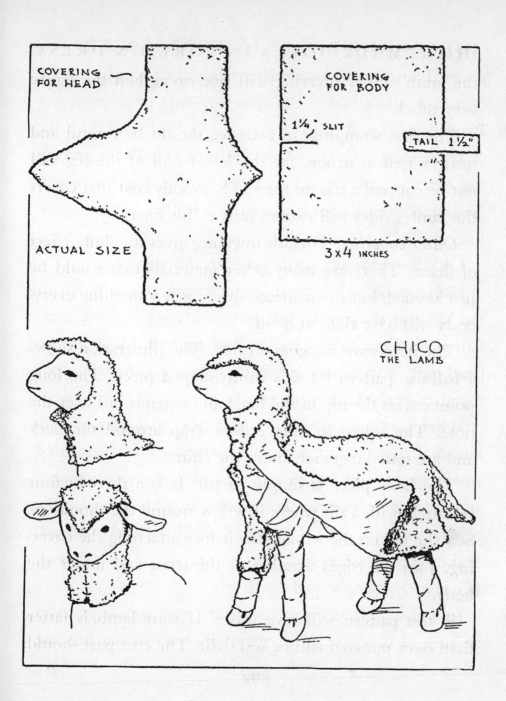

COVERING
FOR HEAD

COVERING
FOR BODY

1¼" SLIT

TAIL 1½"

ACTUAL SIZE

3 x 4 INCHES

CHICO
THE LAMB

the lamb's outer covering will not strengthen the figure very much.

The first wrappings of each leg should be careful and neat as well as strong, for the lower half of the leg will not be covered a second time. The woolly coat that covers the lamb's sides will extend only to his knees.

Outer covering. Turkish toweling gives the fluffy effect of fleece. There are many other materials that would be just as good, but we mention toweling as something everybody will have right at hand.

The head covering goes on first. The illustration shows a full-size pattern for this funny-shaped piece. The long point covers the top of the head and extends out over the nose. The square-looking points wrap around the neck and are sewed together under the chin.

The body piece is simple to cut. It is a three-by-four rectangle with a slit where it wraps around the shoulders. Sew the tail on the wrong side before attaching the covering. Join the edges together at the front and under the body.

A test pattern will save waste. If your lamb is fatter than ours, our coat will be too tight. The coat part should be wide enough at the sides to cover the upper half of the lamb's legs.

There is a fluffy white covering for a lamb which can be used in place of the fitted pieces. We must warn you, though, that it will not prove very serviceable, that is, the lamb cannot be handled much or its position changed often. But anyhow, here it is—cotton. And it really does look lovely!

Under the wrapping of cotton there must be some binding of the legs so they will stand. If you wish to omit the usual wrapping of stocking strips, you can wind string tightly around the legs a few times, then several times around the body.

If you do this part of it well, the lamb with a cotton "dress" can stand and look pretty for a time, at least.

We suspect that an Indian doesn't always fasten a silver bell to his lamb's neck, but we're hanging a bell on our lamb, just the same. It is a small jingling Christmas bell, so Chico "will have music wherever he goes."

Chico can be put to work in other settings besides this one. He would feel at home with Hansel of Switzerland or Angus, the Scotch bagpiper, just to mention a couple of people he would like to belong to. A lamb adds a pleasantly rustic look to any outdoor setting.

In case you want to make a *llama* for your South American setting, we'll explain how; use the same length of wires as for the burro in the Mexican chapter. Also follow the same general plan for making.

The main difference will be in the pose of the head and in the color. You would bend the head wires into a small head. With the head smaller, the neck will be longer than the burro's. Then the neck is bent upright in a haughty manner, instead of forward.

Wrap the llama with tan stocking, instead of black, for the first wrapping. For the outer covering you use the same choice of materials as is suggested for covering the camel, for the llama is the camel's cousin. The camel, El Humpo, will be found posing in the chapter on Arabia.

More things for the setting. A burro, baskets, clay ollas. (Pancho carries an olla on his shoulder in the big illustration.) Deep bowl for pounding cornmeal, leather sandals for Pancho, large-leafed plants of cut-paper to put around the hut.

HENDRIK OF HOLLAND AND THE WINDMILL

HENDRIK of Holland has light skin, rosy cheeks, and fair hair (white sock is what we used) cut in a Dutch bob.

We did not fringe the hair this time because it seems to look all right as it is. But there is no reason why it should not be fringed like that of the other little people in this book.

Hendrik's coat is tight, his pantaloons enormously loose and wide.

His bright blue eyes are painted on with poster color. After it was dry, we decided that we wanted the eyes brighter. So we sewed on two blue beads. In sewing on bead eyes, first push the needle through from the back of the neck to the eye. The bead is caught on the needle and the needle is again brought through to the back and tied. You could sew the thread straight through from the

HENDRIK

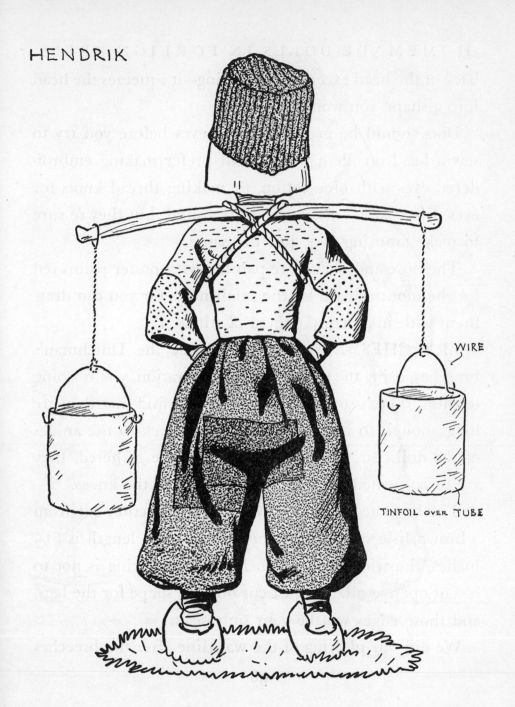

WIRE

TINFOIL OVER TUBE

back of the head except for one thing—it squeezes the head into a shape you won't like.

Dots should be marked for the eyes before you try to sew a bead on. Perhaps you will prefer making embroidered eyes with blue cotton, or making thread knots for eyes. Knots won't always be quite round, but they're sure to make amusing eyes, just the same.

The nose and mouth are painted with poster paint, red for the mouth, black for the small nose. Or you can draw them with ink, or make them of stitches.

BREECHES. After you've cut out the Dutchman's breeches, using the pattern in the illustration, you're going to think there's some mistake. You will find that they are long enough to reach about from the neck to the ankles of the doll. But after the lower edges are gathered, they are to be turned up underneath, about to the knees.

The breeches are made from a whole section cut from a brown lisle stocking (women's size). The length is 6½ inches, the width about 6 inches. The stocking is not to be cut open at all. You just cut out a V shape for the legs, and those edges will be your only seam.

We did our pleating of the waistline after the breeches

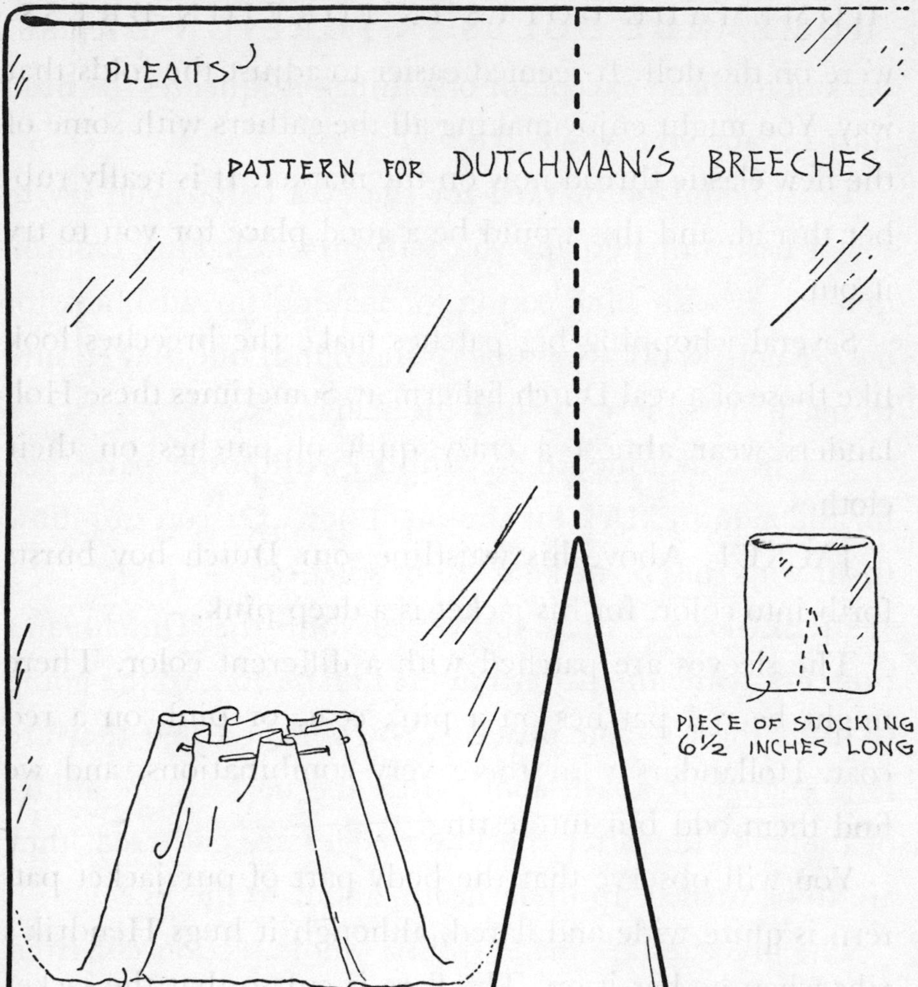

PLEATS

PATTERN FOR DUTCHMAN'S BREECHES

PIECE OF STOCKING
6½ INCHES LONG

TURN UP UNDER

SEAM

GATHERS

CUT AWAY

were on the doll. It seemed easier to adjust the folds that way. You might enjoy making all the gathers with some of the new elastic thread now on the market. It is really rubber thread, and this would be a good place for you to try it out.

Several whopping big patches make the breeches look like those of a real Dutch fisherman. Sometimes these Hollanders wear almost a crazy quilt of patches on their clothes.

JACKET. Above his waistline, our Dutch boy bursts forth into color, for his jacket is a deep pink.

The sleeves are patched with a different color. There might be red patches on a pink coat, or pink on a red coat. Hollanders wear these very combinations, and we find them odd but interesting.

You will observe that the body part of our jacket pattern is quite wide and flared, although it hugs Hendrik's ribs when he has it on. The flare is cut so that the jacket fronts may be crossed for a double-breasted effect.

The goods, folded at the shoulder line, was cut so that front and back are alike. Then we trimmed some off the back piece. The place to trim is shown by a line of dashes

JACKET —

ON FOLD

ON FOLD

PIECED

CUT FOR BACK

SIDE OF HAT
1½" × 5½"

HAT CROWN
1¼" INCHES

on the pattern.

After the jacket was on the figure, we folded the lower edge of it in a sort of hem, to hide its raw edges. It also covers up the gathers at the top of the breeches.

Hendrik's jacket buttons are pins, pushed in at an angle so their points don't stick out. However, this isn't the best way of making buttons. Tiny, real buttons are cute, if you have them. Beads will serve as buttons. Or you can make large, sewed-on knots, or even paint buttons on.

CAP. The cap on Hendrik's head is high, wide, and handsome. It is of maroon-colored corduroy. A nice, soft little cap can be made of cotton stocking. This wouldn't need quite so long a strip because of the stocking's stretchiness. You might like to make another cap, the kind the fishermen wear. It is smaller, and has a peak or visor, like our policeman's cap.

SHOES. A Dutch boy couldn't do much loud clomp-clomping around in the kind of wooden shoes we make for Hendrik. They are tan glove fingers cut as the *sabots* are cut for the French peasant.

There should be socks of some kind—wrapped red yarn, glove fingers, sewed socks, or wrapped strips of color.

Hendrik's stringy little scarf may be made from just about anything—cloth, stocking, yarn.

WINDMILL. Hendrik's home is this red mill with a circle of tulips around its base.

Our little Dutch mill has been kept as simple as possible. There is no balcony, no poles or rigging. Even the wings are not shaped but are perfectly straight strips of cardboard, pasted together criss-cross. You can add all the improvements you like by taking more time to the making.

The suggested body for the mill is a Quaker Oats box, wrapped with red paper which laps about 3 inches at the back.

The roof of the windmill is the easiest roof we ever made! It is just a blue penny balloon, inflated till it's a trifle wider than the box opening. When forced part way into the opening, the balloon bulges, quite like the pictured roofs of windmills.

You can paint shingles on the balloon with brush and ink. And of course you can draw brick lines all over the red wall of the mill, if you wish.

Door and windows are cut from blue or white paper and pasted on. The door is drawn like the old-fashioned

Dutch half-door which was cut in two so the top half could be opened while the lower half remained closed.

Cut-paper tulips (cut in folded strips) are pasted around the base of the mill. If you paste only their lower edges you can bend the flowers out in a pleasing way.

So far, this mill has perfectly straight sides. You may be willing to leave them straight. But if you want to make the sides flare at the base like a real mill, put a wad of cotton under the red paper, at each side, as we show in the small sketch. It is to allow for this that we suggest the 3-inch lap-over at the back. Of course, this wall shaping needs to be done before pasting the lap at the back.

You don't have to have an oats box in order to make a mill, though the box is very convenient. But you can easily make a rolled shape out of cardboard or matstock—or even several layers of wrapping paper.

Our red mill is really red, white, and blue. Red body, white arms, blue roof. In Holland they usually give each mill a name, and you might do the same with your Dutch mill "made-in-America."

In the setting, Hendrik is lying on the dike, sailing his toy boat. The grass that covers the dike and extends back

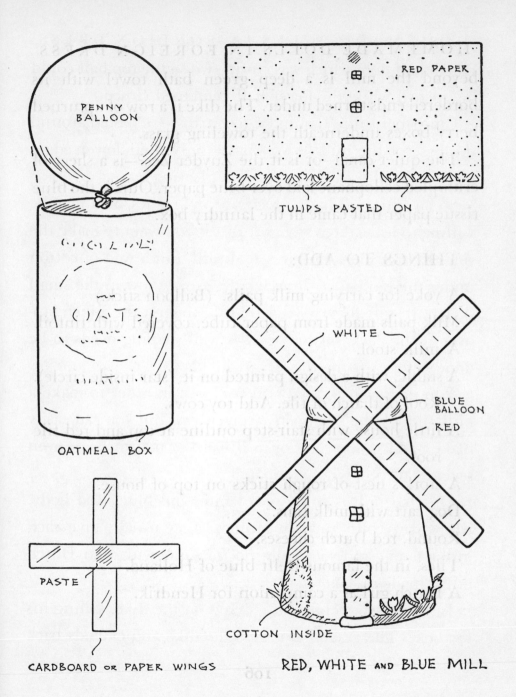

PENNY
BALLOON

RED PAPER

TULIPS PASTED ON

OATMEAL BOX

WHITE

BLUE
BALLOON

RED

PASTE

COTTON INSIDE

CARDBOARD or PAPER WINGS

RED, WHITE and BLUE MILL

beyond the mill is a deep green bath towel with its bordered ends turned under. The dike is a row of upturned berry boxes underneath the toweling grass.

The quiet canal—or is it the Zuyder Zee?—is a sheet of crumpled cellophane laid over blue paper. Ours is the blue tissue paper that came in the laundry box.

THINGS TO ADD:

A yoke for carrying milk pails. (Balloon stick.)

Milk pails made from paper tube, covered with tinfoil.

A milk stool.

A stable, with a design painted on it (star inside circle). Roof of thatch or tile. Add toy cows.

A little house with stair-step outline at top and red tile roof.

A stork's nest of rough sticks on top of house.

Dog cart with milk cans.

Round, red Dutch cheeses.

Tiles, in the famous Delft blue of Holland.

A Dutch girl as a companion for Hendrik.

BOXES

CELLOPHANE

SCOTCH HIGHLANDER

THIS is our Highland laddie, Angus, and his bagpipe. There he stands among the thistles, tootling away.

Angus' hair is sandy in color and a bit curly. Some might call it tousled. His eyes are as blue as the bluebells of Scotland.

In clothing Angus, we have not kept to the costume of any particular Scottish clan. We chose what we thought would be easiest to make, or most interesting, regardless of whether it represented Campbells, Camerons, Macdonalds, or what.

COAT. The coat is of dark, plain-color cotton, with turned-back lapels. It might have a button or two on it, on the front or on the cuffs.

In the pattern, the coat sleeves are amply long, so you can turn back a cuff if you like. Otherwise, cut off the extra

length.

KILT. The kilt—or "philabeg" as Scots sometimes call it—is the pleated plaid skirt worn by Angus. Although our Highland laddie is not a member of the Shepherd Clan, we chose Shepherd plaid gingham for the making of his kilt. Its small, even pattern is easy to press into pleats. If you prefer more color, some dashing plaid of another clan will be more to your liking. The "Royal Stewart Dress" plaid is especially handsome.

There is one thing to watch out for in making the kilt. Although the 3-inch width makes the kilt, it will take quite an astonishing length of gingham because of the pleats. We cannot tell you just how long a strip to cut because different plaids will be pleated differently—but start with plenty!

Beneath his kilt, Angus wears breeches, or "trews," as he would call them. They are short dark trousers which you can cut from any of the trouser patterns in the book.

Angus is almost knee-deep in plaid socks! Each sock is a winding of plaid strip cut on the straight of the goods. When wound spirally around the legs, it gives the diagonal plaid effect you see. The shoes are black cloth, or glove

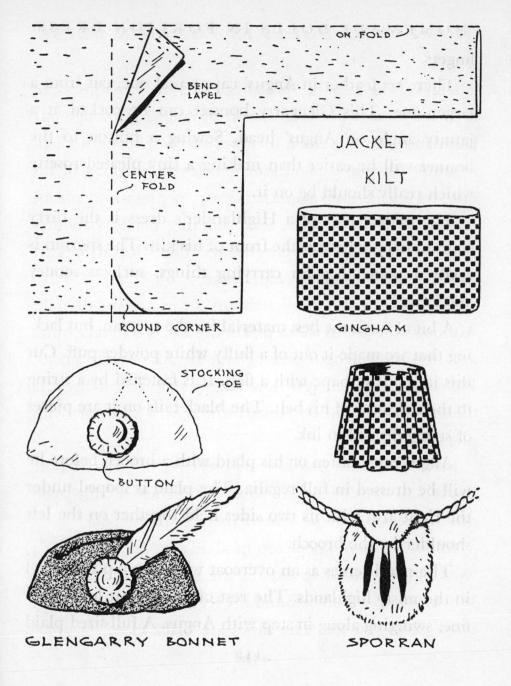

ON FOLD

BEND
LAPEL

CENTER
FOLD

JACKET

KILT

ROUND CORNER

GINGHAM

STOCKING
TOE

BUTTON

GLENGARRY BONNET

SPORRAN

fingers.

There's a feather in Angus' cap, a real one, cut from a larger one. This Glengarry bonnet can be cocked at a jaunty angle on Angus' head. Sewing a button to the bonnet will be easier than making a tiny pleated rosette which really should be on it.

The oddest part of a Highlander's dress is the furry sporran hanging across the front of his kilt. The sporran is really a pouch bag for carrying things, such as money and keys.

A bit of fur is the best material for the sporran, but lacking that we made it out of a fluffy white powder puff. Cut this into a bag shape with a flap. It is fastened by a string to the two sides of his belt. The black tails on it are pieces of string dipped in ink.

Angus must fasten on his plaid with a brooch before he will be dressed in full regalia. The plaid is looped under the right arm with its two sides held together on the left shoulder by the brooch.

The plaid serves as an overcoat when a wrap is needed in the misty highlands. The rest of the time it looks very fine, swinging along in step with Angus. A full-sized plaid

4" WIDE
18" LONG

THE PLAID

seemed too bulky, so we made it only a narrow strip, but its length is correct.

BAGPIPE. The bagpipe that Angus hugs will actually utter a few small squeaks! That is because its mouthpiece is the wooden whistle from a penny balloon.

A real bagpipe is made of animal skin with plaid cloth on the outside of it. Ours is different; it is a bag of plaid stuffed with a bit of cotton, and it's light as a feather.

To make the bagpipe, cut two pieces of plaid from our pattern. Sew them together, leaving two openings as shown. One opening is for the mouthpiece, the other for the finger-keys. Cement on the three little sticks—matchsticks will do in place of the tiny lollipop sticks we used.

Stuff the bag to a soft plumpness with cotton. The bag should be just fat enough to look rounded when Angus carries it squashed down under his arm.

Scots have a funny name for this funny-looking instrument—they call it a "doodlesack."

HOUSE. Angus' home is a stone house with a thatched roof, copied from a house in a village called Thrums.

The one we made isn't really a house, it's only a front! It is a cut-out poster with a box glued to the back. The box

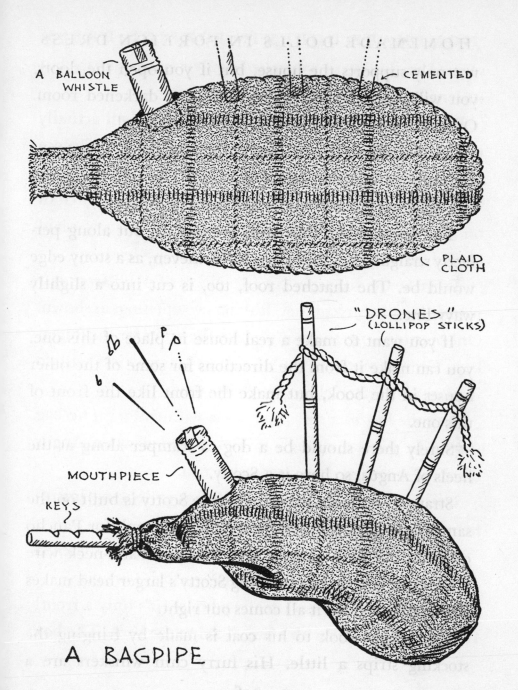

A BALLOON WHISTLE

CEMENTED

PLAID CLOTH

"DRONES" (LOLLIPOP STICKS)

MOUTHPIECE

KEYS

A BAGPIPE

not only supports the house, but if you open the doors, you will see into what appears to be a darkened room. Otherwise you would look straight to nothing!

The house is drawn on heavy gray cardboard. The stones are outlined in either black or white. The roof is colored tan. Shadows painted under the eaves give depth.

The edges of the side walls are not cut out along perfectly straight lines, but are a little uneven, as a stony edge would be. The thatched roof, too, is cut into a slightly wavy line.

If you want to make a real house in place of this one, you can make it from the directions for some of the other houses in the book, but make the front like the front of this one.

Surely there should be a dog to scamper along at the heels of Angus, so here is a Scotty.

Strangely enough, this tough little Scotty is built on the same framework we used for making the lamb for Pancho of Peru, but with shorter legs. The head-and-neck wire is the same length, but bending Scotty's larger head makes his neck shorter, so it all comes out right.

The shaggy look to his coat is made by fringing the stocking strips a little. His furry chin whiskers are a

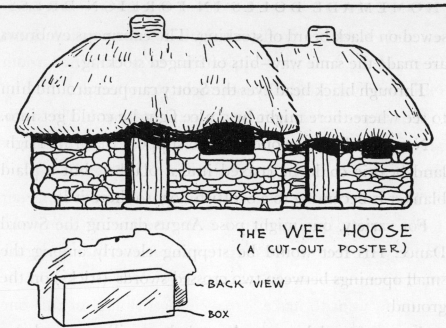

THE WEE HOOSE
(A CUT-OUT POSTER)

BACK VIEW

BOX

BEAD EYES

FRINGED STOCKING

sewed-on black beard of stocking. The enormous eyebrows are made the same way—bits of fringed stocking.

Through black bead eyes the Scotty can peer around him to see where there might be a nice fight he could get into.

Now, we don't for one minute suppose that this Highland beastie could be coaxed into a blanket, but a plaid blanket is becoming to a Scottish dog, so there it is.

For variety, one might pose Angus dancing the Sword Dance. His feet would be stepping cleverly among the small openings between two crossed swords (sticks) on the ground.

A row of medals across Angus' chest will prove what a fine piper he is. You may find some tiny flat buttons, beads, pins, or trimmings that could be fastened to Angus' coat, for medals.

A stone fence (cardboard) and some vines would improve the setting. With a few sheep to guard, Angus could be a little shepherd of the hills, playing his bagpipe for company.

A Shetland pony would make an interesting addition to this setting. The pony would be about like the burro, but plumper. His wrappings would be clipped into a shaggy fringe.

FRENCH PEASANT

GRANDPÈRE is one of the busiest dolls in this book. He is an old French peasant from the Brittany coast.

Grandpère's face covering is of medium tan stocking to give him an outdoor complexion. His cheeks are ruddy (dry rouge put on with the tip of one's finger).

But Grandpère has something that no other manikin in the book has—he has a nose! It's a fat little nose that sticks out in the funniest way! We will tell you more about it later.

His snow-white beard and hair are a stocking toe. If there is a mend in the stocking, you can cut the mend out and allow the hole to be a bald spot on the back of Grandpère's head.

The *sabots* (wooden shoes) could, of course, be modeled from plastic wood, or whittled from any soft wood. But we preferred an easier way to make them. The ones shown were made from two finger cots, those rubber fingers that people sometimes wear over their own hurt fingers. The tips of old rubber gloves will do as well, or even tan cotton gloves.

You can see from the illustrations how they are cut out. The little tabs at the back are joined with rubber cement.

The old gentleman wears jolly red socks (strands of yarn wrapped around his ankles) and rather short blue trousers. We made these of old cotton that was faded to a dim blue.

The toe of a man's blue sock made the soft, squashy beret. The edge is gathered, and is drawn in barely enough to pull the raw edges under out of sight. The beret can be whisked off and on in a jiffy.

In making our smock, we had in mind the enchanting colors worn by Brittany fishermen. That's why we chose for it a rose-red color.

Our smock pattern requires a piece of cotton goods about 9 by 11 inches. Fold it to 5½ inches long. This fold will be the shoulder line. Then fold it down the center and cut like our pattern. Cut in from the side edge for the

GRANDPERE

sleeves. That extra fullness under the arm should be pleated down flat.

Cut an opening down the center front, or cut it open just part way. The sleeves can be gathered or tied at the wrists. You may need to take a small pleat at the back of the neck for better fit, depending on how big your man's shoulders are.

After your manikin is dressed, bend his body so that it has the stooping position of an old, old man.

Now, to get back to the nose. Cut a tiny strip of stocking, tie it in a knot, and draw the knot tight. As you tighten it, push it into a good, lumpy shape. Pin it to the face until you get it sewed all around. Finish by sewing down the two tag ends as smoothly as you can.

Then you must add another head covering to hide this construction work, but this will be only a moment's work. Make a tube of stocking, and gather it around the top just as you did the head in the first place.

Pull the neck fullness toward the back of the head, then tie or sew it. The raw edge at the neck can be concealed under a couple of windings of stocking.

Not all Brittany peasants have black eyes, but ours has.

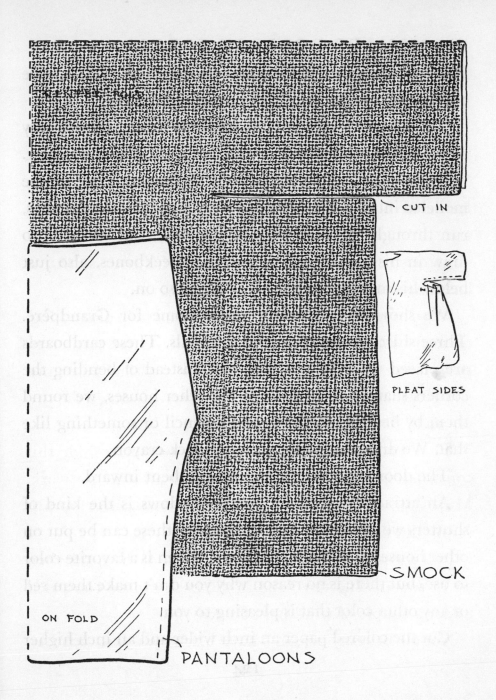

CENTER FOLD

CUT IN

PLEAT SIDES

SMOCK

PANTALOONS

ON FOLD

His eyes are shiny black pins, cut off short with a wire cutter and cemented in with household cement.

The mouth is drawn with ink, just a line, then a very tiny blob of melted red crayon is touched to the center.

If you want to take time to do it, Grandpère's face can be modeled into the character of a weazened old man. Stitches, run through from the back of the neck, can be made to draw in his face a little below the cheekbones, also just below his mouth, around his eyes and so on.

We show here a simply made home for Grandpère. Three shirt cardboards make the walls. These cardboards are placed with the gray side out. Instead of bending the corners sharply, as in most of the other houses, we round them by bending them around a pencil or something like that. We draw the stones on with black crayon.

The door and window are cut and bent inward.

An attractive finish for house windows is the kind of shutters we illustrate. And by the way, these can be put on other houses in the other chapters. Green is a favorite color to use, but there is no reason why you can't make them red or any other color that is pleasing to you.

Cut the colored paper an inch wider and an inch higher

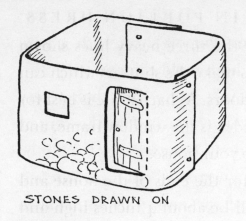

STONES DRAWN ON

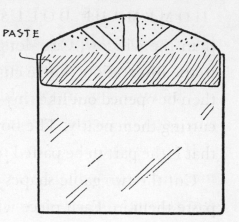

PASTE

MAKING THATCHED ROOF

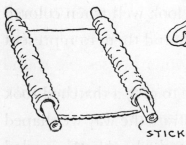

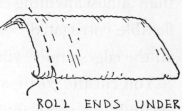

STICK

SHAPING CORRUGATED BOARD

CUT OPEN ON
HEAVY LINES

ROLL ENDS UNDER

SHUTTERS

CLOSED   OPEN

than the window. Cut along the three heavy lines shown in the illustration. These cuts make the shutters which can then be opened out like tiny doors. A sharp knife is best for cutting them neatly. The border is the window frame, and that is the part to be pasted to your house.

Cut the two gable shapes for the ends of the house and paste them in. Each piece will be about 4 inches high and 8 inches wide (or the width of your house wall). Use an inch and a half for pasting, leaving 2½ inches sticking up to hold the roof.

Draw timbers on the end. They look well when colored with brown crayon, with dots all around them to represent plaster.

Thick edges on a roof help more to give a thatched look than almost anything else. We illustrate the way we shaped flexible corrugated board for a thatched roof. We curled all the edges under, you see.

You cut the corrugated board about 3 inches larger all around than you want the finished roof to be. Moisten the board a little all over, quickly. It softens at once. Then roll one edge over a round stick such as a broomstick or a shade roller. Let it dry.

Although you lay the piece of board flat except for the roll at the edges, it will not dry quite flat, but will be rather uneven-looking. This only adds to the finished effect of thatch. Some of the little ridges will mash down, too, but that won't hurt anything.

When the board is dry, it is sometimes necessary to straighten out the top edge a little so it will fit over the other half of the roof at the ridge. You can moisten that edge ever so little, lay a ruler along it and let it dry again.

Although all this sounds complicated in print, the actual work is very little trouble and takes but little time to do. The drying is all that takes time, but you can be doing something else while the drying is going on. When the corrugated pieces are dry, they keep their shape.

Both sides, as well as the eaves and ridge of each roof piece should also be rolled under to make the roof look thick. A notch needs to be cut at each corner to fit it under, or you can cut off a little of the corner.

To further imitate thatching, strings can be tied across it in a couple of places, though we did not do that on ours.

A much more substantial house can be built from a carton. Then you could roll up many little balls of clay, flatten them against the carton and have quite a realistic stone house. For this house a real thatched roof could be made. Materials might be raffia, broomstraws, grass, straw, soda straws, moss, fringed wrapping paper—any of these.

In our setting, a thatched stable snuggles up against the house, French style. The peasant usually has such a small patch of ground that he has to group his buildings closely to leave room for his garden.

The stable is a carton with its front mostly cut away. The manger is cardboard, bent and tied with two strings to hold its angle. It could be pasted to the stable wall, or attached with a couple of two-legged paper fasteners. Fill it with hay (grass, excelsior, broomstraws). A few wisps of hay on the stable floor help give a natural effect.

Grandpère's spading fork is a paper picnic fork with parts cut away. We would have preferred one of those flat wooden spoons for making a spade, but we didn't have one, so we made this pitchfork-sort-of-thing instead.

The dug-up dirt pile is a heap of dried tea leaves. One could just as well use dried coffee grounds.

The flagstones are irregular gray cardboard shapes cut from shirt boards. When they are laid in sand, the effect is very good.

AUBERGE

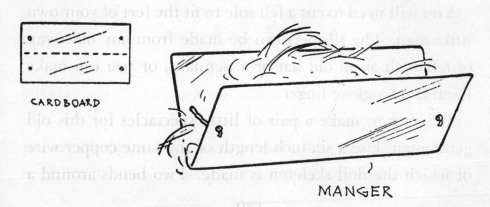

CARDBOARD

MANGER

The sign *"auberge"* means that Grandpère's home is an inn where passers-by may find meals and lodging for the night.

The Lombardy poplar tree is another of those balloon stick trees made like those in the Swedish chapter.

There are many other things you can add to improve this setting. Instead of digging, the old gentleman might be shown out walking with a cane, or mending a blue fishing net, or just resting on a big stone beside his door. You might pretend that he was watching the fishing fleet come in.

In case you want Grandpère to take his ease beside his doorway, you can make him a pair of comfortable slippers to wear instead of the *sabots*. You will find a slipper pattern on one of our pages.

You will need to cut a felt sole to fit the feet of your own little man. The slippers can be made from any old scrap of felt such as an old hat or a pennant, or you can make them from a glove finger.

It is fun to make a pair of little spectacles for this old gentleman. Use a six-inch length of the same copper wire of which the doll skeleton is made. Two bends around a

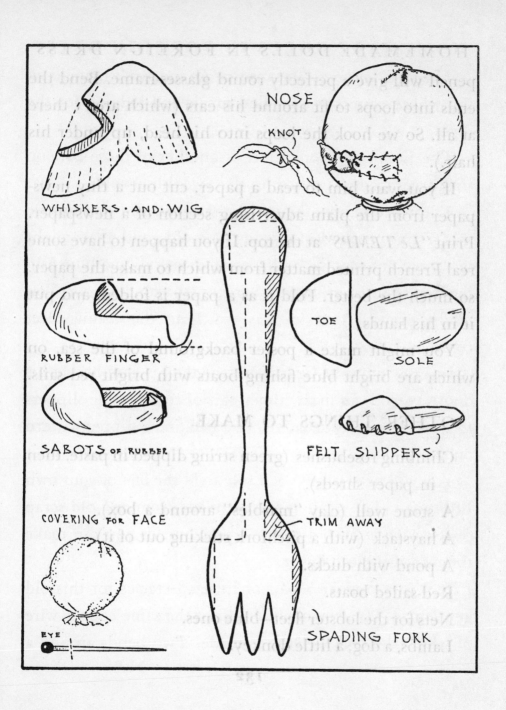

NOSE

KNOT

WHISKERS · AND · WIG

RUBBER FINGER

TOE

SOLE

SABOTS OF RUBBER

FELT SLIPPERS

COVERING FOR FACE

TRIM AWAY

EYE

SPADING FORK

pencil will give a perfectly round glasses-frame. Bend the ends into loops to fit around his ears (which aren't there at all. So we hook the loops into his head, up under his hair.).

If you want him to read a paper, cut out a tiny newspaper from the plain advertising section of a newspaper. Print *"Le TEMPS"* at the top. If you happen to have some real French printed matter from which to make the paper, so much the better. Fold it as a paper is folded, and put it in his hands.

You might make a poster background of the sea, on which are bright blue fishing boats with bright red sails.

OTHER THINGS TO MAKE.

Climbing rosebushes (green string dipped in paste, then in paper shreds).

A stone well (clay "marbles" around a box).

A haystack (with a pitchfork sticking out of it).

A pond with ducks.

Red-sailed boats.

Nets for the lobster fleet—blue ones.

Lambs, a dog, a little donkey.

SWEDISH GRETA

THIS is Greta of Sweden, daughter of Vikings. But Greta is not a wanderer like her Viking ancestors. She is too busy at home, churning and sweeping, and baking flat bread in sheets as thin as a cracker.

We wanted to make Greta a true blonde—as blonde as she could possibly be. So instead of using stocking for her body covering, we used knitted silk underwear of a delicate pinky tint. This gives Greta the peaches-and-cream complexion we think she should have. We made her cheeks rosy by a careful rubbing of dry rouge on a wad of cotton.

Her bright blue eyes are two beads we happened to have. Otherwise we'd have painted the eyes with blue poster paint or embroidered them with embroidery cotton, a large blue knot for each eye.

We made a pure white wig. You may prefer to use a

pale tan stocking instead of white. The two fat braids make Greta look like a little princess of olden times.

When a Swedish maid puts on her best holiday finery, she is as colorful as a gipsy. More so, really, because she is so spotlessly clean.

Greta's snowy blouse was cut like the pattern, and made from the most filmy white stuff in our scrap box. The blouse opens down the center of the front.

The oddly shaped sleeves were gathered at the wrist but the gathers were not drawn up until after the blouse was on. Even the billowing skirt for this little person takes only a bit of goods, 12 inches by 4½ inches.

If you want to add a trimming band to the skirt hem, here is the way to make a gorgeous, shining band. Paste on cellophane Scotch tape. It is the quarter-inch width sold for gift wrappings. You don't moisten it; it has its own moist "stickum" right on it. You can get this tape in different colors.

As Greta's costume is the actual costume of one Swedish village, we are telling you just what those colors are, in case you want an authentic costume. But there are many others —charming ones, too—that are quite different. One of these

has an apron with flowers splashed all over it.

Greta's quaint striped apron has wide bands of red, with narrow bands of white, blue and green. In this village, the girls believe that wide stripes bring riches, so they wear the broadest bands of color they can find.

The flowery kerchief is the corner of a handkerchief, a two-for-five handkerchief from the dime-store. It is thin enough to drape well.

Don't forget to add shoulder straps, made like suspenders. They fasten to the top of the girdle. A scrap of narrow flowered ribbon is just the thing for the straps.

The girdle of this costume is usually quite a deep color—dark red or green, so it contrasts with the whiteness of the blouse and the brilliant apron. Even the one-inch width may make too wide a girdle for your doll, but you can trim it to fit. It is finished off with criss-cross lacings.

We like that funny little cap! It is too small to really fit on her head, so it is fastened on the back. But what it lacks in breadth, it makes up in height.

This peaked cap is made from a two-by-four bit of ribbon, silk, or velvet, rolled into a steep cone. Two streamers are sewed on the back. This cap is red, but after Greta

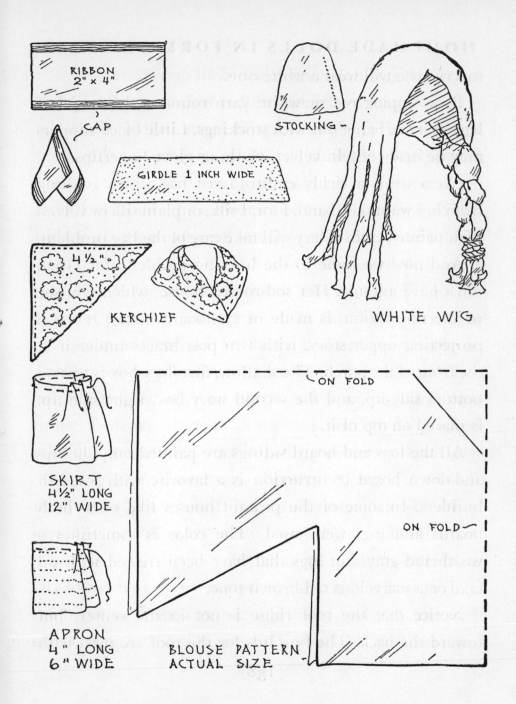

RIBBON
2" × 4"

CAP

STOCKING

GIRDLE 1 INCH WIDE

4½"

KERCHIEF

WHITE WIG

ON FOLD

SKIRT
4½" LONG
12" WIDE

ON FOLD

APRON
4" LONG
6" WIDE

BLOUSE PATTERN
ACTUAL SIZE

marries she will wear a white one.

By wrapping red or white yarn round and round her legs, you can fit her out with stockings. Little black slippers may be made of felt, velvet, cloth, or glove fingertips.

Greta wears a richly embroidered bag which is slung from her waist on a band. Floral silk, or plain silk or velvet, with painted embroidery will take care of the bag problem.

And now we come to the housing problem, for Greta must have a home. Her sod-roofed house, which you see in the illustration, is made of cardboard boxes. It has a projecting upper story, with two post braces under it at the front of the porch. The shallow, first-floor box is turned bottom side up, and the second story box, right side up, is placed on top of it.

All the logs and board sidings are painted on. The up-and-down board construction is a favorite with Swedish builders. In some of the peasant houses like ours, both boards and logs were used. The color is sometimes a weathered gray, but logs that have been treated with oil take on a marvelous red-brown tone.

Notice that the roof ridge is not in the center, but toward the back. The box lids for the roof are used with

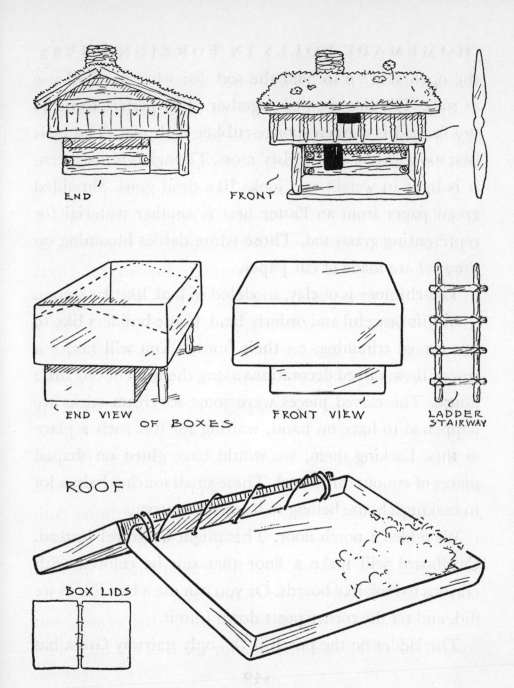

END   FRONT

END VIEW   FRONT VIEW   LADDER
OF BOXES   STAIRWAY

ROOF

BOX LIDS

the open side up to hold the sod (or what we shall use as sod). The lids are tied together. The perfect thing to use for sod is a green sponge-rubber bath mat. The next best sod we know of is florists' moss. Though it is not green, it is light in weight and looks like dead grass. Shredded green paper from an Easter nest is another material for representing grassy sod. Those white daisies blooming on the roof are made of cut paper.

The chimney is of clay, modeled to look like flat stones.

In this peaceful and orderly land, house-builders like to put carved trimmings on their houses. You will notice a row of these carved decorations along the front of our little house. The carved pieces were some ice-cream sticks we happened to have on hand, waiting for just such a place as this. Lacking them, we would have glued on shaped pieces of cut-out cardboard. These small touches help a lot in making a house belong to its own country.

We added a porch floor. This might be gravel instead. Cardboard will make a floor that can be colored with crayons to look like boards. Or you can use a box lid, as we did, and set the corner posts down into it.

The ladder on the porch is the only stairway Greta has

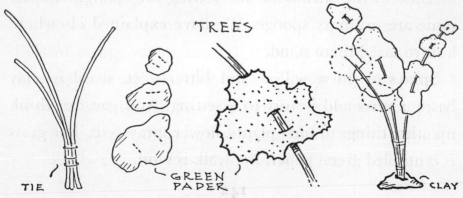

TREES

TIE

GREEN
PADER

CLAY

159

to get up to her little room under the roof.

Since Sweden is so famous for its trees, we must have plenty of them in our setting. One way to make a tree is to tie together three long balloon sticks. Cut two of them to a shorter length. No two should be the same length. To give them a graceful curve, soak them in hot water till you can bend them as you want to. When dry, they retain their curve. The illustrations show plainly how the clumps of delicate green foliage are made and put on. These clumps, too, should vary in size, no two the same. The edges of the clumps can be shaped into as lacy a design as you care to put on them. A lump of green clay no bigger than a golf ball can be pinched into a base that will hold up a three-branched tree. If you put lots of leaf clumps on each limb, you might need to add a little more clay to the base.

Some of the shrubs in our setting are sponge rubber, some are ordinary sponge. We have explained elsewhere how to make them stand.

Sprays of pussy willow and bittersweet, stood in clay bases, always add beauty to a setting. And you can think up other things to add—plants, flower sprays, etc. The grass is crumpled green paper, the walk is sand.

In the setting, Greta is seen sweeping with a homemade broom such as Cinderella might have used. It is made of long grasses so firmly tied together that the broom never comes apart. Down south, in our own America, brooms exactly like it are made and used today. You can make the broom of grasses or old broomstraws, and place it in Greta's hands, as we did. Or let her churn, if you'd rather.

The churn in our picture wasn't really "made" at all. It is just the core of a string ball from the grocer's large ball of twine. The dasher is a skewer. It is brightened up with dashes of color.

Did you wonder how we turned Greta's head so she looks away from her churn? A pin did it, a pin at the back of her neck. Sometimes it takes two pins, if they are short ones. You can turn her head in different directions and make it stay there.

ANGELO OF ITALY

NOT only is Angelo made of stocking, but he's dressed in stocking, too. He is playing a tune on a straw flute. There's a bright flower in his hat. This is one of the very small flowers sometimes found in hat trimmings. Angelo might have several little flowers in his coat lapel, too.

A pin is pushed through each of Angelo's hands and on into the straw flute, so he can hold it. There is a row of tiny openings snipped along the length of the flute.

Angelo has medium tan skin and bushy, curly hair. He wears three times as many wigs as the other dolls; that's why he has three times as much hair. The first wig is cut the largest, then a smaller wig goes over it, and a little wig tops the other two. All are fringed, all are very black.

Ordinarily, snipped fringe hair curls up whether you want it to or not. But one of our wigs did not curl after it

144

BOX

GREEN
BATH-
MAT

was fringed, so we wet it and hung it over a golf ball to dry. The ball was placed on the mouth of a bottle so the hair could hang down. Before leaving it to dry, we fluffed the ends up. When dry, the hair was curly.

In one picture Angelo isn't dressed yet! He holds up one shoe as though he were saying, "Mother, am I to wear these shoes again today?" We show him partly dressed so you may see how a manikin's body may be shaped up with a little padding here and there.

The chest has cotton padding beneath its wrappings; the back has a small round pad of cotton. The thighs could have been padded with cotton, but we did it with extra wrappings of stocking strips.

Angelo's white undershirt is a piece of white stocking 2½ inches long, 4 inches wide. This is folded at one side, sewed along the other. The blue shorts are made with a fold at one side, seam at the other.

Angelo wears a silver medal (a circle of tinfoil on a thread). You might make him a pair of tiny earrings of gold tinsel cord, but they probably wouldn't show much because of his hair.

Angelo's big black eyes are two big black pins, cut short

MEDAL

PIN

THREE
WIGS

WHITE
SHIRT

BLUE
SHORTS

FOOTSTOOL

and cemented in. He has eyelashes, too (ink lines).

The sash and socks are made from pieces of striped sock—red and white. The sash is really a sort of extra.

The little black boots need no explaining. They are made like the socks, only shorter. You could give them thread shoelaces.

Beneath one of Angelo's feet there's a footstool. It is a large, colored milk bottle cap with a cushion of patterned silk, stuffed with a dab of cotton.

To make Angelo's peaked hat, cut off the toe of a stocking about two inches from the end. Then push and pull it until you find the shape you like. Roll it up here, pull it down there—you can coax it into many hat shapes. It can be any color you like.

Angelo's clothes should not be too brilliant in color. We made his coat black, his hat tan, and the trousers blue.

In making the trousers, use the tip of a stocking toe. This will make a well-shaped waistline for the boy. The only seam is along the inside of the legs.

If you should be lucky enough to have some cast-off socks (about 4-year-old size), then you can make trousers with an elastic belt. You can either cut away part of the

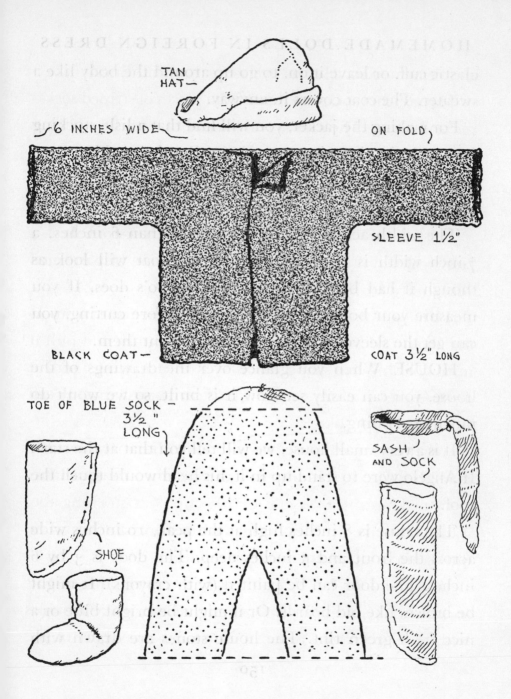

TAN HAT—

6 INCHES WIDE

ON FOLD

SLEEVE 1½"

BLACK COAT—

COAT 3½" LONG

TOE OF BLUE SOCK— 3½" LONG

SASH AND SOCK

SHOE

elastic cuff, or leave it on, to go up around the body like a sweater. The coat covers it, anyway.

For making the jacket, you will find that a lisle stocking (women's size) is easiest to work up. Cut the stocking open along the seam. Fold it for the shoulder line and cut out a jacket something like our pattern.

The width across should not be less than 6 inches; a 7-inch width is better. Otherwise the coat will look as though it had been outgrown, as Angelo's does. If you measure your boy from wrist to wrist before cutting, you can get the sleeves just the length you want them.

HOUSE. When you glance over the drawings of the house, you can easily see how it is built, so we won't do much explaining.

It is a very small house, we will tell you that at the start. If Angelo were to stand up in it, his head would touch the roof.

The house is 8 inches high at the peak, 10 inches wide across the front and 5 inches deep. The door is 3 by 6 inches. The door can be painted (with crayons). It might be brown, like old boards. Or it might be bright blue or a nice fresh green tint. The house stones are drawn with

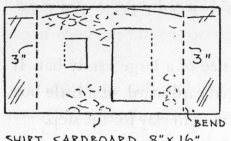

3"   3"

SHIRT CARDBOARD 8"x16"

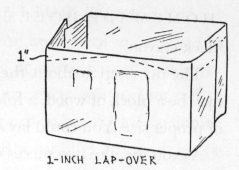

1"

1-INCH LAP-OVER

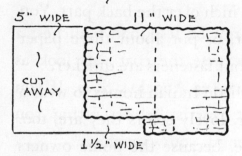

5" WIDE   11" WIDE

CUT
AWAY

1½" WIDE

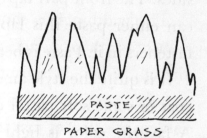

PASTE

PAPER GRASS

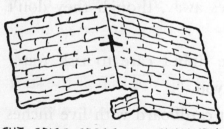

CUT CRISS-CROSS FOR CHIMNEY

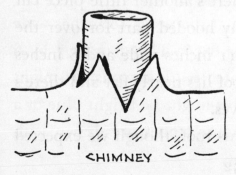

CHIMNEY

STONE WALL

BOARD

CLAY   PEBBLES

black crayon.

The doorstep is about the size of a large candy bar. It may be a block of wood, a folded cardboard, or a little box of proper size. You could lay stones in clay for the step.

As you see, the two pieces of the house are joined at the sides. The front part laps one inch over the back part. You can either paste this lap-over, or put about three paper fasteners in it. Paste is better but fasteners are quicker.

It is quite the style among little Italian homes to wear a coat of some soft pastel color, lovely colors they are, too. A favorite color is light blue, because the home owners think that blue keeps the flies away, though they don't seem to know why.

In painting our house, we didn't care to risk water colors, so we tinted it with crayon.

The pink tile roof is a shirt cardboard with five inches of its length cut away. Also there's another little piece cut out, where you make the tiny hooded part for over the doorway. The actual roof is 11 inches wide and 8 inches deep at the wide part. The roof lies nearly flat and there's almost no overhang to the eaves.

We decided on paint for this roof, though we expected

it to curl all out of shape. It did, too, but only while it was wet. When dry, it had straightened itself out very well.

Here is how we did it: first we wet the roof all over, then quickly brushed vermilion poster paint over it with an old toothbrush. After most of the excess water (and a lot of the color) had dripped off, we tried some finger painting on the moist surface, by making finger tracks across it in rows, like the tile pattern. Then we stood it straight to dry, which it did in a short time.

Next we drew some loose, wiggly lines with black crayon to represent the tiles. The color is now a very nice pinkish tint, and is not at all even, but we didn't want it to be perfectly even. The homemade tiles on ancient peasant houses of Italy are never the same in color, so everything worked out as we wished.

The roof can be fastened to the house from underneath with any kind of adhesive tape, gummed envelope flaps, or pasted strips of paper.

It is always easy to make a chimney for a toy house from a large cork, a spool, a roll of paper, corrugated paper, or a piece of balsa wood shaped to fit the slope of the roof. Or you can do as we did—use a small cardboard roll that came from inside a ball of kite string. A criss-cross cut in the roof allows the chimney to be poked through from beneath.

It will be worth your time to make a base for this rather frail house. Cut a piece of heavy corrugated board to fit inside its lower edge. A piece 5 by 10 inches allows our house to be set around it just as you set a cover over a box.

Whether you glue the house to its base or not depends upon what you mean to do with it. Suppose you want to furnish the house with table, bench, and spaghetti bowl. Then pin the house to the base. Otherwise, you can glue the walls fast to the base and your house will be quite firm and strong.

A little house standing by itself is rather a forlorn and lonesome-looking thing. You will want to put in some grass, green paper strips of grass. Paste them around the base of the house, but if you paste only the bottom of the grass stems, they can lean outward in a natural manner.

Several layers of grass and tall plants look very nice indeed. The tallest ones go at the back, of course. When all are pasted and dry, you can bend their tops away from the house. Flowers can be pasted around among the leaves, for color.

This setting is an excellent place for some of those green string vines we've mentioned before. Wet with paste, dipped in tiny bits of green paper, they can be twined or pasted here and there. Colored confetti dots could be pasted on as flowers.

Everyone loves the idea of a little house tucked away in a crease in the hills. We couldn't quite manage that, but we did give the house a green hill of its own to stand on. Here it may perhaps overlook the famous Tiber River, or the bright blue Bay of Naples.

This green hill is a green sponge-rubber bath mat draped over a box, with a few crumpled newspapers in front of the box to make the hill a little less steep. A green bath towel could be used instead of the mat.

In making up one of your own settings, you may find a place for a fragment of stone wall. You can make this out of a board or cardboard box by spreading modeling clay over it and sticking pebbles around in the clay. A few larger pebbles, imbedded in clay, might be grouped around the base. They will give extra width to the base and aid it in standing firmly.

You can poke some little red poppies (on wire stems)

into the clay, and let them grow from crannies in the stones, as they do in Italy.

OTHER THINGS TO MAKE FOR AN ITALIAN SETTING:

A stone bench (cardboard across two spools).

A fountain and statues (soap sculpture carvings).

Lambs—any number of them.

A little donkey (like the burro).

A brightly decorated cart with big wheels.

A gondola.

Grapevines strung among little poles.

Parasol pines (tube of paper with foliage wrapped in one end. Other end pushed down over cork that is nailed to a base).

A poster background of Vesuvius spouting fire, the beautiful Bay of Naples in the foreground.

SWISS CHILDREN AND THEIR CHALET

HANSEL is fair-skinned and blue-eyed. He has a short haircut; his wig is very light tan or white stocking. His body is padded out a little more than some of the other manikins.

Hansel wears festival dress consisting of a black velvet suit and a white blouse. The suit is richly embroidered. Each coat lapel bears a white edelweiss design, and a line of zigzag trimming runs around the edge of the jacket.

On many materials we can paint designs with poster paint. Or we can do all of it with embroidery threads—not all the small design shown in the illustration, but we can make dots, crosses, and other small forms.

The jacket pattern shows both halves of the jacket—one half is the cutting pattern, the other half shows how the jacket is made up, with puffed sleeves and a rounded lapel.

Buttons ornament both sides of the jacket.

Although we call it a black velvet suit, it need not be velvet or velveteen. Any black goods may be used, even black stocking if need be.

Speaking again of the decorations, on some materials paint is all right, and you can stamp tiny designs with a matchstick. Dip it in poster paint and stamp it down, varying the designs by whittling the stick into different-shaped points.

For materials that do not take kindly to poster paint, try making dot designs with a heat-softened crayon. Heat the crayon with a match and touch it to the material. It leaves raised dots of color. Sometimes this method comes in very handy.

Hansel's white blouse has long sleeves which he often wears rolled up as you see them. This means that his arms must be smoothly wrapped with the stocking strips with which they are covered.

We do not show Hansel wearing his fancy suspenders because his coat is in the way. But we have drawn them for you on another page, showing all kinds of designs that you might use. Don't try to show them all, you won't have

HANSEL

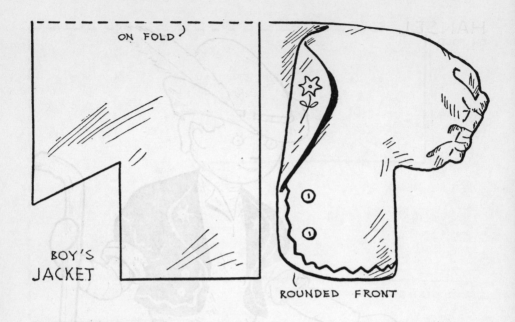

BOY'S JACKET

ON FOLD

ROUNDED FRONT

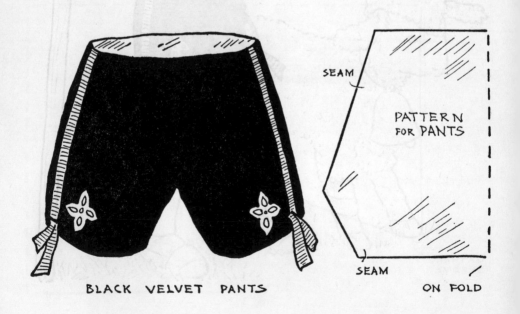

BLACK VELVET PANTS

SEAM

PATTERN FOR PANTS

SEAM

ON FOLD

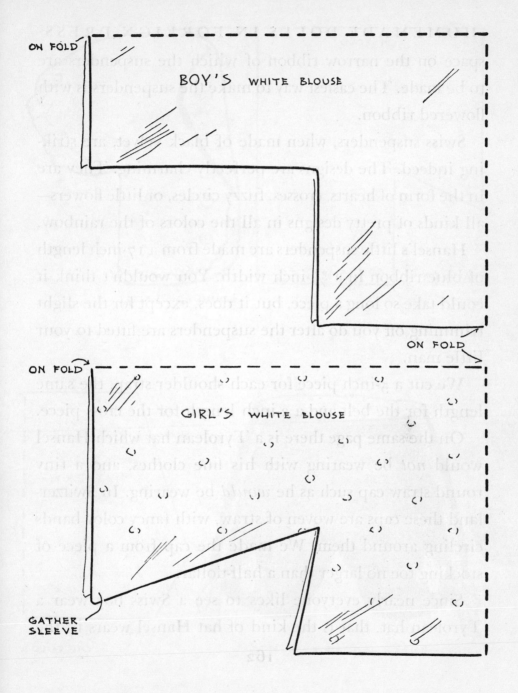

ON FOLD

BOY'S WHITE BLOUSE

ON FOLD

ON FOLD

GIRL'S WHITE BLOUSE

GATHER
SLEEVE

space on the narrow ribbon of which the suspenders are to be made. The easiest way to make the suspenders is with flowered ribbon.

Swiss suspenders, when made of black velvet, are striking indeed. The designs are perfectly charming. They are in the form of hearts, crosses, fuzzy circles, or little flowers— all kinds of pretty designs in all the colors of the rainbow.

Hansel's little suspenders are made from a 17-inch length of blue ribbon in a ⅜-inch width. You wouldn't think it could take so long a piece, but it does, except for the slight trimming off you do after the suspenders are fitted to your little man.

We cut a 5-inch piece for each shoulder strap, the same length for the belt and a 2-inch length for the cross piece.

On the same page there is a Tyrolean hat which Hansel would *not* be wearing with his fine clothes, and a tiny round straw cap such as he *would* be wearing. In Switzerland these caps are woven of straw, with fancy color bands circling around them. We made the cap from a piece of stocking toe no larger than a half-dollar.

Since nearly everyone likes to see a Swiss boy wear a Tyrolean hat, that is the kind of hat Hansel wears in the

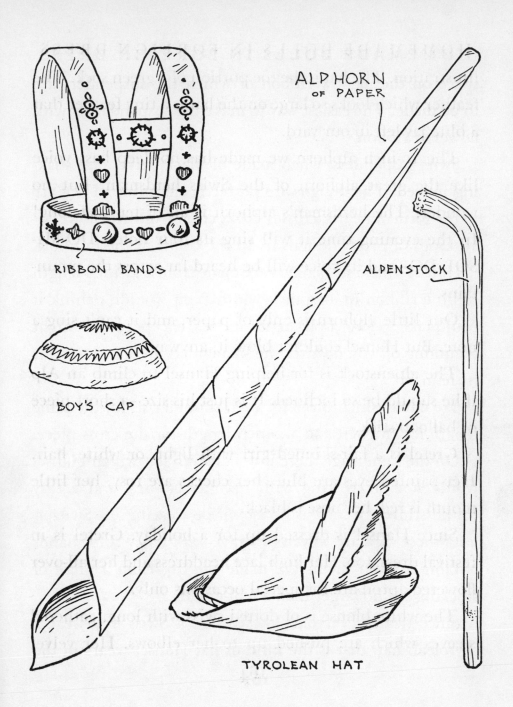

ALP HORN
OF PAPER

RIBBON BANDS

BOY'S CAP

ALPENSTOCK

TYROLEAN HAT

illustration. The hat is the toe portion of a green sock. The feather which looks so large on the hat is a tiny feather that a blue jay left in our yard.

The 10-inch alphorn we made has no deep bass voice like the great alphorn of the Swiss herdsman. But no wonder! The herdsman's alphorn is all of ten feet long! In the evening time it will sing its four notes—DO-MI-SOL-DO—and its voice will be heard far across the mountains.

Our little alphorn is only of paper, and it can't sing a note. But Hansel couldn't blow it, anyway.

The alpenstock is for helping Hansel to climb an Alp if he should be so inclined. It is just his size—a short piece of balloon stick.

Gretel is a fair-skinned girl with light, or white, hair. Her painted eyes are blue, her cheeks are rosy, her little mouth is red, her nose is black.

Since Hansel is dressed up for a holiday, Gretel is in festival dress, too. Her high lace headdress and her all-over flowered apron are for special occasions only.

The white blouse is of dotted swiss with long, gathered sleeves which are pushed up to her elbows. Her velvet

girdle is black and her skirt is of dark silk. A little piece of black velvet ribbon will make a fine girdle. But the important thing is that it should be black whether it is of velvet or not.

For the silver button-like ornaments you could use beads, painted dots, or embroidered knots. The crossed lacings can be represented with threads.

It took about 6 inches of black lace to make the shirred headdress. This lace was simply sewed to the top of the doll's head, but it really should be attached to a tiny black cap.

The Swiss miss wears her heavy silver chains swinging at her side instead of wearing them as necklaces. We sewed the two chains to the top of the girdle, under the arms.

That long chain is a piece of beaded pull chain from a lamp. The short one is a string of steel beads.

The earrings are two round necklace clasps. You could use beads, instead. Small beads can be quickly threaded on a fine wire to make jewels for these little people.

Gretel's flowered apron comes nearly to the hem of her dress. Although real Swiss aprons are of silk, we made ours of voile.

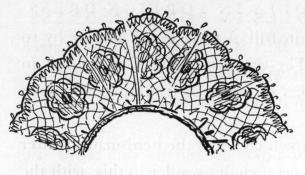

BLACK LACE HEADDRESS

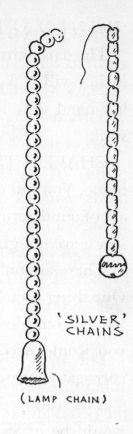

'SILVER' CHAINS

(LAMP CHAIN)

FLOWERED APRON

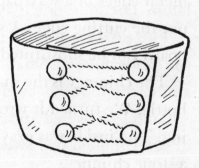

BLACK VELVET GIRDLE

The dark skirt is quite full. A piece of silk about 5 by 10 inches will make it. The tiny posies that Gretel holds in her hand were leftovers in a box of trimmings and such stuff.

CHALET. This brown chalet is the herdsman's winter home. You can construct a chalet similar to this, with the aid of our descriptions for making other houses in the book, so we are not giving any illustrated details for this house.

There are only a few points that are different about it. One thing is the wide roof with stones on top to keep high winds from blowing the roof away. Because of the stones you would need rather heavy cardboard for the roof, or corrugated board.

The scalloped border along the roof is not carved, as it would be in Switzerland. We made the border from the metal edges of a wax paper box. This was the inner edge, not the cutting edge. A scalloped edging of paper or cardboard can be substituted for the metal.

The chimney is the small outside carton that held an ink bottle. We turned it wrongside out, to be rid of the printing. The inside was gray, just what we wanted for making a stone chimney.

The Swiss are great woodcarvers, and their balconies are

STONES ON ROOF

BOTTLES

FENCE (CARDBOARD)

seldom without interesting carved designs. We made the balcony from part of a cardboard laundry box. The design on the railing is drawn with crayon.

To attach the balcony to the house, we cut four tabs at the back, having left on two extra inches for that purpose. Two of the tabs were turned *upward* against the house and pasted; the other two were turned *downward* and pasted.

The windows are not cut in, but are pasted on underneath green shutters. You will find the making of window shutters fully explained in the French Peasant chapter. There would be several windows overlooking the balcony, but we merely indicated them.

If you wonder why the clothesline is up on the second floor, we'll tell you. The downstairs is used as a wood shed and stable, as is often done in Switzerland, and the family lives upstairs.

This is quite a large chalet, and it requires large boxes or cardboards for its making, but it will be easy for you to make a small one, with fewer windows and with only a tiny balcony up under the eaves.

The woodpile is a heap of twigs cut into lengths. The bench is of cardboard (it could easily be of wood), and the milk cans are small, fat bottles covered with tinfoil. The pans are bottle caps, also covered with tinfoil. Hansel is in the picture, too, bustling about doing his chores.

One could build a stone fence to put around the chalet, using clay and pebbles. Or make a picket fence like ours, from long and short strips of cardboard. The short strips are cut pointed, for pickets, and are pasted to the long ones. Small wooden posts or little cardboard boxes will serve to support this fence.

Sand and gravel form the ground near the chalet. On the walls there clings a vine of green cord, with shreds of paper for leaves. The background is a large poster of snow-covered Alps.

POSSIBLE ADDITIONS:

A knapsack for Hansel.

Skis (long pieces of wood with upturned ends).

Flower boxes to put outside chalet windows.

Painted Swiss designs on chalet.

A churn, butter pails, and tubs; more milk cans.

A stable, haystack, scythe, rake.

Sheep, goats, cows—all with bells on.

Wood carvings.   171

It would be interesting to make a goat, with cotton for its covering. Use the same foundation as for the lamb described in the chapter about Pancho of Peru. Wrap the body and legs with cotton, and pull some tufts of cotton loose, like goat hair. Ink splotches would make a black-and-white goat.

Little wire horns would be added, and possibly a fine wire in the tail so you could bend it out in the funny way that goats carry their tails.

ARAB SHEIK

SHEIK ABOU BEN is an Arab. But because he is a Bedouin Arab, he is always traveling. A Bedouin's home is wherever he may pitch his black tent. The very name, Bedouin, means a dweller in tents. Any Bedouin would feel insulted if you were to call him a house-dweller.

Our Arab should have a tall, lean appearance, so we made his head a bit smaller than the other dolls' heads. The smaller the head, the taller a figure will appear to be.

The skin color of Abou is dark tan. He has beady black eyes, so what could be more proper than to make them of black beads? You can get the same effect with black-headed pins, clipped off and cemented in place.

The mustache, nose, and eyebrows are black stitches. The beard is a crescent of black stocking fringed and sewed to the face.

A Bedouin's headdress, or *kaffeyeh,* is a folded cloth held on by a thick band of goats' hair or wool. We made the headdress from a 7-inch square of flimsy white chiffon handkerchief, bordered with green cellophane tape. The band is emerald green yarn caught at front and back with two stitches and one bead. Crimson yarn, too, looks well on this dark-faced fellow.

An Arab's clothing is simple. There is the dark, heavy wool *burnoose,* or over-robe. Under this is worn a flowing white robe, sometimes belted, sometimes not. In drawing patterns for the two robes, we drew one pattern on top of the other.

Abou's burnoose is in bold stripes and bold colors. It was a 5¼ by 14-inch piece of old sateen. There is a 2-inch opening for the arms, and the burnoose is left open a little way up each side seam, about a half-inch or so. We fringed all raw edges.

A genuine burnoose has a large, pointed hood at the back, made all in one with the robe part, but the kind we illustrate is also worn by Arabs as an outer garment.

Soft white goods 15 by 9½ inches makes the long inner robe. We have made the pattern to include extra long

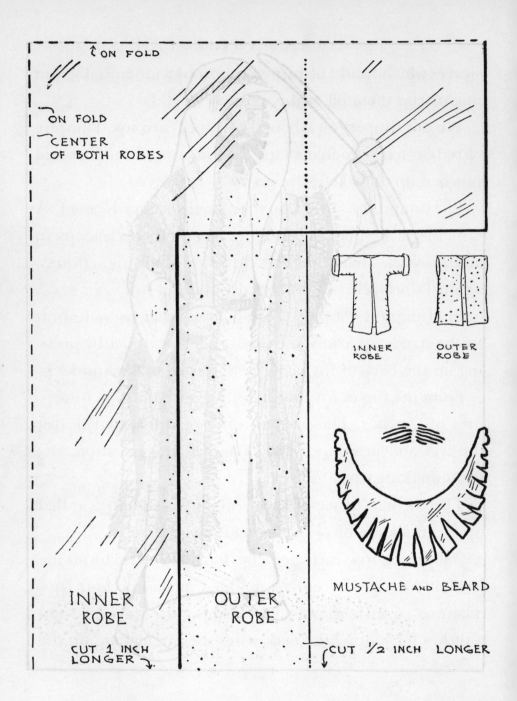

↑ ON FOLD

ON FOLD
CENTER
OF BOTH ROBES

INNER
ROBE

OUTER
ROBE

MUSTACHE and BEARD

INNER
ROBE

OUTER
ROBE

CUT 1 INCH
LONGER

CUT ½ INCH LONGER

sleeves which would be turned back into wide cuffs. Or you might trim them off at the wrist, as we did.

We put slippers on Abou. Their toes turn up. They are of red Scotch cellophane tape, bound around the foot and pinched up to make the points.

El Humpo is a dromedary, or single-humped camel. A camel is, at best, an odd-looking beast. His neck loops in and his back arches out; yet, in spite of all his ugliness, a camel's neck curves into a really graceful line.

El Humpo is not pretty, but he does what we want him to—he stands up firmly and poses. We found that by pressing on the back of his neck, we can even make him kick!

From the top of his hump to the floor, our camel measures $9\frac{1}{2}$ inches. The body is a roll of corrugated board, the legs and head are wires. The padding is cotton, the wrappings are stocking.

The corrugated paper body ($5\frac{1}{4}$ inches long) is rolled up to a thickness of $1\frac{3}{4}$ inches and tied securely.

Cut three wires, each 30 inches long. One wire forms the head and neck. The others, doubled, make the four legs. There is a 1-inch allowance for joining the leg wires, and 2 inches for joining the neck wires. Before making up the

camel figure, study the drawings of the burro in the chap
ter about Mexican Pedro for more complete explanations.

We gave the leg wires a good twisting together to make
them more rigid. The legs are 6½ inches long. Bend the
ends of the legs into wire loops 1 inch long. If El Humpo
is to be a "ship of the desert," he needs big feet.

It usually takes a little juggling to bend the feet so that
all four rest evenly on the ground. But you can depend
on the leg wrappings to help out.

Arrange a goodly wad of cotton for the hump. You can
wrap it loosely to the body with a few strips, to hold it in
place for the later wrappings.

Pad and wrap the head; stuff and wrap the neck. (See
burro illustrations.)

For the camel's outer wrappings, you have a considerable
choice in materials. Best of all is some sort of tan-colored
knitted wear, for it will stretch into shape beautifully.
Woolly knitted scarf or sweater material will make excellent covering. These materials could be cut into rather
wider strips for the wrapping.

Any of the following materials may be used: tan stocking, old Turkish toweling or cotton flannel (dyed in tea),

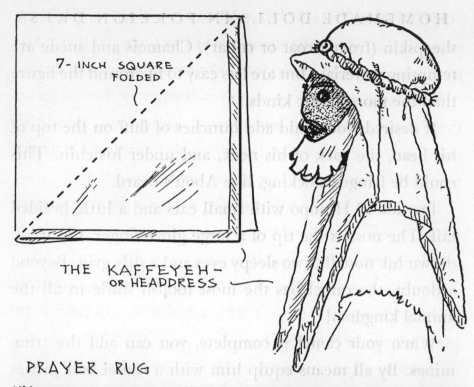

7- INCH SQUARE
FOLDED

THE KAFFEYEH —
OR HEADDRESS

PRAYER RUG

sheepskin (from a coat or collar). Chamois and suède are tempting materials, but are less easy to fit around the figure than the more elastic kinds.

If desired, you could add bunches of fluff on the top of his head, the back of his neck, and under his chin. This could be fringed stocking, like Abou's beard.

Provide El Humpo with small ears and a little braided tail. The nose is the tip of a large glove finger. On it are drawn ink nostrils, two sleepy eyes and a silly grin. Beyond a doubt, the camel has the most foolish smile in all the animal kingdom!

When your camel is complete, you can add the trimmings. By all means equip him with a camel bell just as though he were the chief camel of a whole caravan. A tiny, tinkling Christmas bell on a red string will be right.

You can also drape him with a string of blue beads as the Arab does. This is the Arab's talisman to protect his camel against sandstorms, bandits, and the Evil Eye.

Add a blanket of brilliant color, perhaps in rainbow stripes.

In posing the camel, you will find that he stands better when his neck is curled back towards his body—a typical

camel pose. If you bend his neck outward, his front legs must be braced forward to balance him.

A camel figure, or three camels with the Wise Men, make an impressive Christmas setting. The clothing of the Wise Men would be just like that of Abou.

It is not a magic carpet you behold on our page but a Prayer Rug. Five times each day Abou kneels on it, with its point toward the East—toward Mecca—and says his prayers.

Our rug was a scrap of chair upholstery in a small geometric pattern. All we had to do to it was fringe its three raw edges and outline the prayer-rug shape with a single black thread.

One could make a lovely rug out of velveteen, with designs painted on with poster color. Remember that a prayer rug always has some sort of a pointed design at one end.

Our date palm has tissue paper leaves, a balloon stick trunk, and a green clay base. When placed near a radiator, the leaves stir and wave in the breeze, for all the world like a real tree in a real breeze. A cluster of ripe dates is drooping from its top.

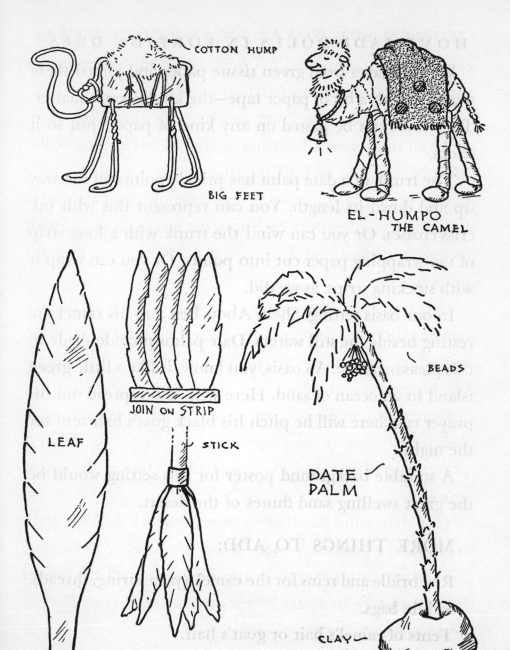

COTTON HUMP

BIG FEET

EL-HUMPO
THE CAMEL

LEAF

JOIN ON STRIP

STICK

BEADS

DATE
PALM

CLAY

We cut leaves from green tissue paper and joined them together with a bit of paper tape—the kind doesn't matter. The leaves can be pasted on any kind of paper, just so it sticks.

The trunk of a date palm has prickly points all the way up and down its length. You can represent this with ink criss-crosses. Or you can wind the trunk with a long strip of tan wrapping paper cut into points. Or you can wrap it with stocking strips, as we did.

In our oasis setting, Sheik Abou Ben and his camel are resting beside the still waters. Date palms provide shade in this pleasant place. An oasis, you know, is like a little green island in an ocean of sand. Here will Abou spread out his prayer rug, here will he pitch his black goat's hair tent for the night.

A suitable background poster for this setting would be the great swelling sand dunes of the desert.

MORE THINGS TO ADD:

Red bridle and reins for the camel (yarn, string, thread).
Saddle bags.
Tents of camel's hair or goat's hair.

A goatskin water bottle (of dark kid glove). These water bottles, as well as the camel's hair tents, were used by Abraham and Jacob away back in Bible times.

Rugs and brilliantly striped blankets.

Bales and bundles in gay wrappings.

Sheep with black faces.

Our Bedouin Arab's full name is Sheik Abou Ben Adhem and he is named in honor of one who loved his fellow man—may his tribe increase! And so, because Abou is a friend, he makes salaam (right hand to forehead as he bows) and says, "Salaam," meaning "peace and safety" to us all.

WONG SU OF CHINA

WONG SU is a Chinese fisher boy whose only home is his sampan, or covered boat.

When Wong Su goes ashore with his catch of fish, he carries them in two baskets slung from a carrying pole. If he gets a chance, he will do coolie work—carrying people's bundles on the ends of his carrying stick.

We are told that the word "coolie" means "bitter strength," and this is easy to believe when we see the size of the bundles some of the coolies carry.

Although our Wong Su's clothing is cotton goods of a light color, there is no reason why it couldn't be almost any quiet color, either light or dark.

The patterns for the clothes are those used for our own manikin. We suggested a side opening for the coat, but this was only to give variety.

The trousers are cut to hang loosely on the figure, loose and baggy. The drawings of the coolie hat just about explain themselves. We made the hat of paper, but a piece of old straw hat would be even better. Straw should be wet before you attempt to cut it out and sew it in a lapped-over seam.

The lines drawn on our hat were to make it look like rice straw hats worn by peasants. The better Chinese coolie hats are woven from thin strips of green bamboo. One of these hats may easily outlast its wearer.

The soles of Wong Su's sandals are of cork, like those of the Japanese girl's sandals. Here we use cork to represent the thick layers of cloth or felt of which Chinese soles are made. The upper can be made of cloth, stocking, or part of a glove.

A poor coolie would scarcely be wearing embroidered sandals, but we put a few dabs of paint "embroidery" on just the same.

We gave Wong Su's wig a rather short haircut with uneven edges. At the back of the head he wears a black yarn queue, shown in one small sketch.

Notice that he wears an elephant charm—a lucky ele-

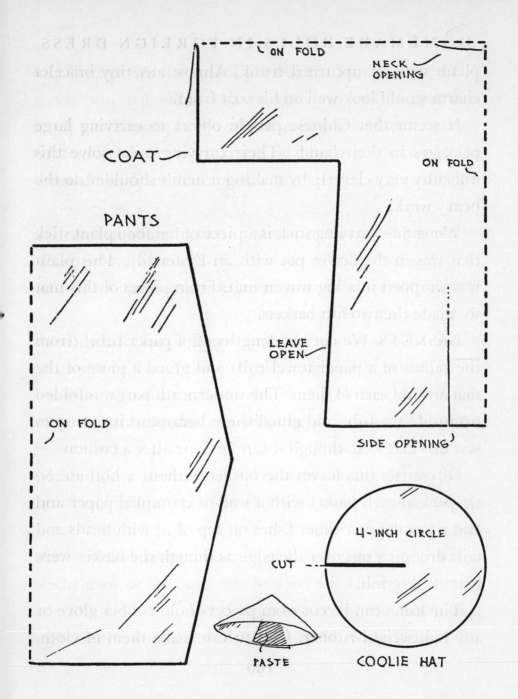

ON FOLD

NECK
OPENING

COAT

ON FOLD

PANTS

LEAVE
OPEN

ON FOLD

SIDE OPENING

4-INCH CIRCLE

CUT

PASTE

COOLIE HAT

phant with an upturned trunk. Almost any tiny bracelet charm would look well on his coat front.

It seems that Chinese people object to carrying large packages in their hands. Their carrying poles solve this difficulty very cleverly by making a man's shoulder do the heavy work.

Wong Su's carrying stick is a piece of bamboo plant stick that was in the flower pot with an Easter lily. This plant was wrapped in a big woven mat. From pieces of this mat we made the two fish baskets.

BASKETS. We cut two lengths off a paper tube (from the center of a paper towel roll) and glued a piece of the mat around each of them. The underneath part was folded up inside the tube and glued there because it isn't easy to sew this mat well, though it can be done after a fashion

Of course, this leaves the basket without a bottom. So we packed each basket with a wad of crumpled paper and laid a few floppy rubber fishes on top of it, with heads and tails drooping out over the edge as though the basket were brim full of fish.

The fishes can be cut from pieces of old rubber glove or any lightweight rubber. Or you can make them of cloth,

BLUE PAPER UNDER
CELLOPHANE

PAPER
CUP

CHINESE BUCKET

old gloves, or paper.

In place of fish, Wong Su might be carrying baskets of tea (dried tea leaves) or he could carry wrapped bundles, as in the little picture.

SAMPAN. Perhaps sampans were once made of three boards, since that is what the word means, but nowadays they are made of many boards instead of only three.

These hooded boats are used a good deal for ferrying people across rivers. But on some sampans there are families living—families who have never lived on land at all.

Our cardboard sampan points upwards at the ends, and as the bottom is flat, the boat stands without any base under it.

It is ten times as easy to make a sampan as it is to explain the making of it. We could make a half a dozen of them in the time it takes to explain one.

The building material is a shirt cardboard. Perhaps almost any piece of cardboard of the same size would do, but shirt boards are handy. You can dip them in water and shape them in all kinds of ways. When dry, this board holds its form with very little pasting or fastening.

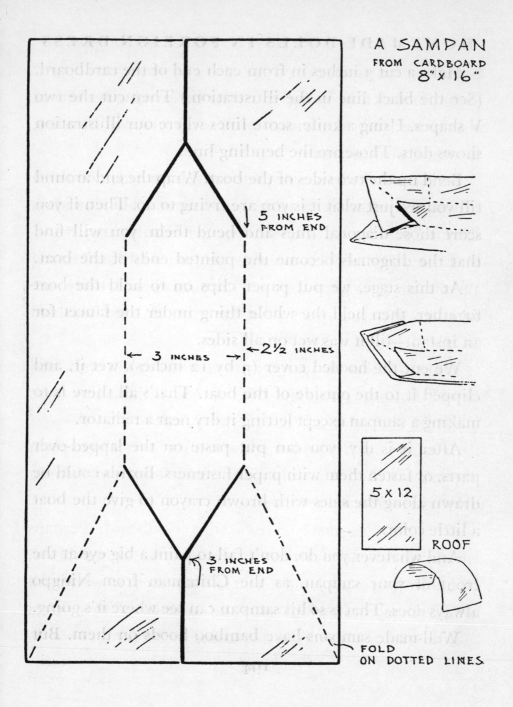

A SAMPAN

FROM CARDBOARD

8" X 16"

5 INCHES
FROM END

3 INCHES

2½ INCHES

5 x 12

ROOF

3 INCHES
FROM END

FOLD
ON DOTTED LINES

Make a cut 3 inches in from each end of the cardboard. (See the black line in the illustration.) Then cut the two V shapes. Using a knife, score lines where our illustration shows dots. Those are the bending-lines.

Bend up the two sides of the boat. Wrap the end around till you see just what it is you are trying to do. Then if you score those diagonal lines and bend them, you will find that the diagonals become the pointed ends of the boat.

At this stage, we put paper clips on to hold the boat together, then held the whole thing under the faucet for an instant—till it was wet on all sides.

We cut the hooded cover (5 by 12 inches), wet it, and clipped it to the outside of the boat. That's all there is to making a sampan except letting it dry near a radiator.

After it is dry, you can put paste on the lapped-over parts, or fasten them with paper fasteners. Boards could be drawn along the sides with brown crayon to give the boat a little color.

And whatever you do, don't fail to paint a big eye at the front of your sampan, as the Chinaman from Ningpo always does. That is so his sampan can see where it's going.

Well-made sampans have bamboo hoods on them. But

many sampans have a framework over which are spread pieces of matting. Sometimes there are many pieces of different sizes.

We spread a scrap of cloth over the hood as matting. But you could use some of the same plant mat as that used for the baskets. Lay other small pieces of mat inside the sampan to give a lived-in look.

A tiny box lid or two can be set inside the boat to serve as a little deck, or as table or seats. You can see Wong Su's rice bowl and chopsticks on his table.

A short piece of bamboo plant stick becomes a fishpole. The bag-shaped fishing net, which will trail behind the boat, is a scrap of lace net.

Nearly every sampan has a collection of bamboo poles slung along its sides. These are for fishing, for the hanging of washing out to dry, and for boosting the sampan around in shallow water. You can tie on a few twigs or thin sticks as poles.

As to the pole that Wong Su is wielding, it's not a pole at all, but a soda straw!

SETTING. The river on which the sampan is resting might be the Yangtse or the Hwang-Ho. We made it of a sheet of glistening clear cellophane over blue paper. Blue cellophane over white would do just as well. The wiggly water lines are drawn on the under paper.

The Chinese bucket is a cut-down Dixie cup. Crayon lines indicate boards and hoops. A soda straw handle goes through two punched holes. A bucket would be of use on a sampan, no doubt.

We have a good reason for suggesting that you tie up a number of little cloth bundles and stow them in the sampan as cargo. Not only will they give an important air, but they will help prop Wong Su up! Then he can stand without a base. Of course, you can always pin his feet to the boat, but bundles of cargo look better.

If you want to be good to Wong Su, why not outfit him with gay clothes for celebrating his great holiday, New Year's? It will give you a chance to work up some of the loveliest pieces of silks you can find. You can embroider designs on them, make little thread frogs for the fastenings, and top him off with a round cap with a great tassel dangling from its center.

A sample color scheme: trousers of violet; emerald or jade green jacket with gold threads (Christmas cord); a crimson skullcap with long turquoise blue tassel. If the cap had a red bead at the top in place of the tassel, it would mean that its wearer is a married man.

OTHER SUGGESTIONS:

Bright banners lettered with Chinese characters.
A little kite of bright paper in the form of bird, butterfly, eagle, man, or dragon.
A lantern or two (see Japanese lantern).
A rudder for the sampan.
Wheelbarrow, sedan chair.
A temple.
Bales of silks.
Firecrackers.

You will enjoy the job of making up a name for your own China boy. Such names as Wun Chin, Hop Long, Hou Kum, all sound much like real Chinese names. Wang, Mister Wu, Ting Ling—you can think them up by the dozen and have a good time doing it.

HINDU LADY

MUMTAZ is only eight inches tall, but she's every inch a lady. Dusky tan is the color of her complexion. Her eyes and lashes, her eyebrows and nose are all black; her mouth is red.

A piece of soft silk sock about 3 by 8 inches makes her sleek black hair. This piece is wrapped around her head, drawn smoothly to the back and twisted into a knot. It is pinned or sewed in place.

The sari and gems of a Hindu lady are perhaps the first things we notice about her garb. The sari is a long, gauzy veil, hand-painted in fantastic designs and brilliant colors. On sheer material, the strong colors become softer in tone.

A real sari might be as much as five yards long and a yard wide. It wraps around the lady's waist, with one long end trailing to the ground. The other end is swathed

around her head and chest, with its corner tossed over her left shoulder.

Our small sari is in the same proportion as a grown-up one, which makes it 5 by 24 inches in size.

Material should be the thinnest, softest stuff you can find: chiffon, veiling, net, gauze, cheesecloth, or fine curtain net.

Here's a clever trick for making filmy material easier to handle and giving it a bright border at the same time. It is Scotch cellophane tape in quarter-inch width, a gift-wrapping tape sold at gift counters and stationery stores. It comes in various glossy colors, also in gold and silver, and costs 10¢.

Attach a band of this tape to the goods in a 5 by 24 inch rectangle before cutting the goods to size. Next, tack the goods on a board with thumbtacks while you paint on the decorations. Then cut the goods and tape together. Or, if you prefer a very narrow band, cut through the middle of the tape.

This cellophane trimming provides a colorful, satiny border for the sari, and at the same time prevents the edges from fraying.

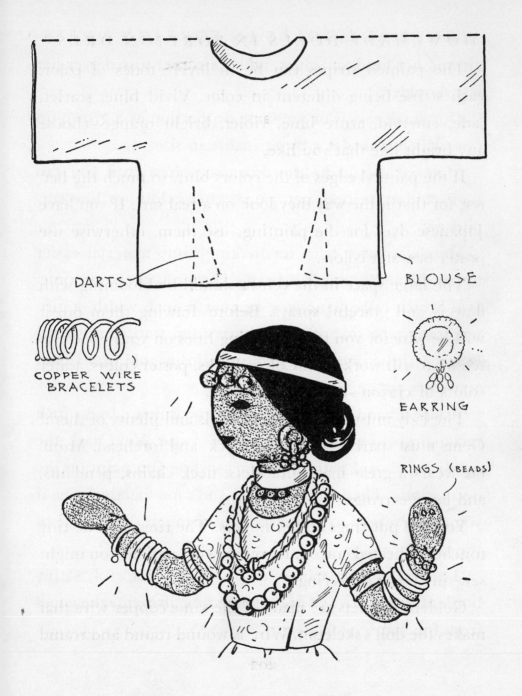

DARTS

BLOUSE

COPPER WIRE
BRACELETS

EARRING

RINGS (BEADS)

The painted stripes can be in lovely tones of color, each stripe being different in color. Vivid blue, scarlet, jade, emerald, azure blue, violet, bright orange—choose any bright hue that you like.

If the painted edges of the colors blur, so much the better, for that is the way they look on a real sari. If you have Japanese dyes for the painting, use them, otherwise use poster or water colors.

The large space in the center should be blooming with flowers and graceful sprays. Before drawing them on, it will be wise for you to try drawing lines on your goods, to see what will work best. Colored inks, poster colors, water colors or crayon—use any of these.

The lady must have flashing jewels and plenty of them! Gems must sparkle from arms, neck, and forehead. Mumtaz wears a great many bracelets, neck chains, pendants, and large earrings.

You can put rings on her fingers. The rings will be tiny touches of heated crayon. If you are very patient you might sew tiny beads on as rings.

Golden bracelets are made of the same copper wire that makes the doll's skeleton. Wire is wound round and round over a pencil, and there you have a whole armload of bracelets in a jiffy!

The earring shown is a bright button with threaded beads swinging from the button's eye. Beads or rolled-up pieces of tinsel cord can be made into stunning earrings. One of Mumtaz's glistening necklaces is of tinsel cord, the other of beads.

Around her head is a jeweled band with bead dangles falling over her forehead. The band is narrow ribbon, tinsel ribbon, or fancy cord.

We may as well mention that Mumtaz would doubtless be wearing toe rings and anklets on bare feet instead of such slippers as we have placed on her. But little red slippers with upturned points can be quickly made by wrapping around each foot a bit of the shiny tape used on skirt and sari.

A waist for Mumtaz should be snug-fitting and short-sleeved. Our pattern is plenty large and will need fitting. The sleeves will no doubt need to be shortened a little, depending on the length of your doll's arms.

Handy patterns can be cut from Kleenex (double, as it comes from the box). You can fit it around the figure as you would fit the softest of soft cloth. The doll-figures vary in size; that is why a fitting is advisable.

The waist should be a bit loose around the body, then nipped in with the darts indicated on our pattern. Darts will help to give shape to the figure.

An opening cut down the center (either front or back) makes the waist easier to put on. We made our waist white, but it could be of light, dark, or bright colors—any color that looks well with the skirt.

We made a gathered skirt of rose-color voile. Its hem is bordered with a double row of the same Scotch tape trimming we put on the border of the sari.

Mumtaz is shown grasping a Punjabi fan in her hand. A drawing of the fan shows about how it is made. The paper part is cut double, wrapped over the handle, and pasted. Fine ink criss-crosses give the effect of basket weaving.

The toothpick handle has on each end a little blob of orange crayon. Heat the end of the crayon till it forms a drop, and dip the ends of the toothpick in it.

You will find it easy to create a lovely little garden pool. In it there can be real water and real plants or flowers.

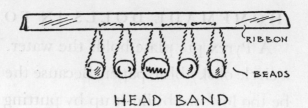

RIBBON

BEADS

HEAD BAND

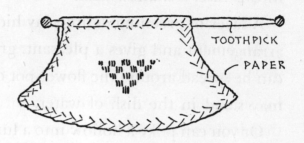

TOOTHPICK

PAPER

PUNJABI FAN

SARI
5" x 24"

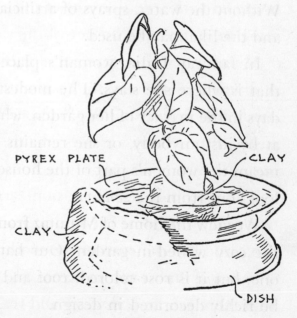

PYREX PLATE

CLAY

CLAY

DISH

GARDEN POOL

A Pyrex pie plate holds the water. Beneath the plate is a circle of sky blue paper. Because the plate by itself would be too low, we build it up by putting something under it, in this case, a shallow dish.

A layer of green modeling clay hides the outside of the arrangement and gives a pleasant, grassy color. More clay can be spread around the flower pot of whatever plant you may stand in the dish of water.

Or you can poke a hollow into a lump of clay, fill it with water and stand fresh flowers in it, or grasses or leaves. Without the water, sprays of artificial flowers, bittersweet, and the like may be used.

In faraway India, woman's place is in the home and that is where she stays. The modest Mumtaz spends her days in the privacy of her garden, where she can't be gazed at by just anybody, or she remains in the *zenana,* which means the women's part of the house. The grilled balcony looks out from the *zenana.*

We view the home of Mumtaz from the side overlooking the cozy walled-in garden. Our hatbox house is a plain one, but it is rose-colored, roof and all! The walls are to be richly decorated in design.

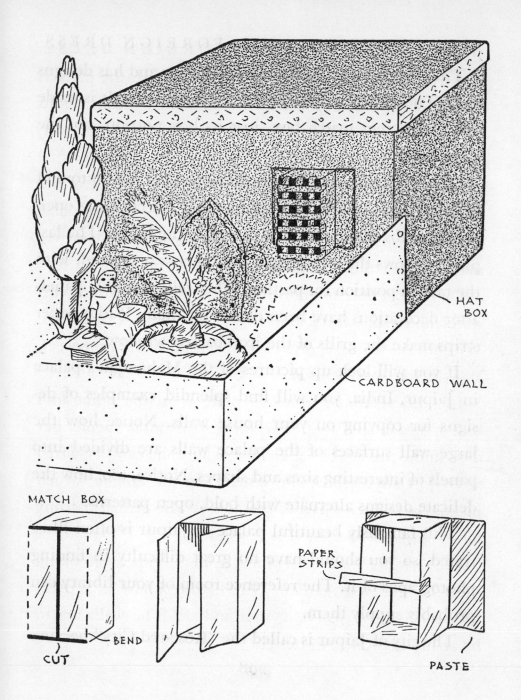

HAT
BOX

CARDBOARD WALL

MATCH BOX

CUT

BEND

PAPER
STRIPS

PASTE

The door is an arch of pasted-on paper and has designs on it. The grilled balcony is like a bay window. It is made from a five-cent match box, just its box portion, not the outer part.

Our first small picture shows how you cut the bottom of the box. The second picture shows how the cut parts open out into tabs which are to be pasted to the house. The last picture shows the box turned the other way around, with the tabs in position for pasting. They will resemble panels after decorations have been drawn on them. White paper strips make the grills of the iron-barred window.

If you will look up pictures of the Maharajah's palace in Jaipur, India, you will find splendid examples of designs for copying on your house walls. Notice how the large wall surfaces of the palace walls are divided into panels of interesting sizes and shapes. Notice, too, how the delicate designs alternate with bold, open patterns.

This famously beautiful palace of Jaipur is often illustrated, so you should have no great difficulty in finding photographs of it. The reference room of your library can probably supply them.

The city of Jaipur is called the "Rose-red City" because

of its many pink-and-white buildings and paving.

One of the nice things about a hatbox house is that it may have rooms inside, and furniture, and little people. You lift the lid, and there you have a bird's-eye view of the small folk in their own home.

If spare hatboxes were more plentiful, we would be making many of our houses from them. A carton can be made into a house very much like the one shown, with a large cardboard laid over it for a roof. It would have the same pink paper covering, the same balcony and designs. If you were lucky, you might find some scraps of figured wall paper that would make a satisfactory outer covering for the house.

A walled-in garden gives a delightful air of mystery to a scene like this. You make the wall of cardboard, which may be colored pink to match the house. Several shirt cardboards can be joined for making a wall.

Vines would look attractive clambering over the wall from within. There is, in the garden, a cardboard bench for Mumtaz to sit on while she contemplates the pool and its flowers.

The tree is of green paper, very dark green if you wish

to call it a cypress tree. The tree trunk is a tube of tan wrapping paper, rolled round and round a clump of cut paper leaves. A clay base holds the tree upright, while sand covers the base.

A nice addition to the setting would be one or two Numdah rugs with their large designs of bird, leaf, flower, and tree-of-life. One rug would be laid on the bench for Mumtaz to sit on; the other would be placed at her feet.

Numdah rugs are white with fringed edges all around. The colors in their designs are strong, cheerful colors—emerald, orange, crimson, etc. You can sometimes find pictures of these rugs among the house-furnishing advertisements in your newspaper.

JAPANESE GIRL

HER name is Kiku, which means Chrysanthemum, but the courteous way of addressing her is to call her O-Kiku-San, meaning Miss Chrysanthemum.

Kiku wears no hat, but carries a paper parasol with a flower design on it. When she goes out she does not carry a handbag, for her long sleeves form two pockets in which she can carry many small articles.

When she plans to carry large parcels from the store, her shopping bag will be a square of cloth. She will knot its four corners together, put her parcels inside and carry it in her hand or over her arm.

MAKING THE DOLL. The doll's outer covering should be light tan stocking—not too dark—for the Japanese are not a very dark-skinned race. The complexion color of the Japanese royal family is said to be pale ivory.

HOMEMADE DOLLS IN FOREIGN DRESS

O-Kiku-San's hair is as black as night. Her wig is made as described in the first chapter. But there is that tuft on top of her head which must be explained. Cut a 2-inch square of black stocking, fold and slit it along the fold. (This is done just as the lantern paper is cut. See the lantern illustration.) Pucker two edges together into a little clump and sew to the head.

Little girls don't *really* wear their hair in a topknot in Japan—only ladies do. But we are letting O-Kiku-San play lady because she looks so cute. Besides, Japanese doll-makers often make girl dolls' hair this way.

Dressing a Japanese doll is a delightful pastime! The kimonos are lovely, and they are ever so easy for us to make. A narrow strip makes the sash (or obi), a big cork makes the pair of amusing little sandals. With the obi tied in a butterfly bow at the back, Kiku will look beautiful either coming or going!

Japanese clothing is simpler than ours. The outer dress is a kimono. The underdress is also a kimono, and this one is often more brilliantly colored than the outside one. No buttons, hooks, or clasps are needed, for the obi holds everything in its proper place. Boys and girls dress much

SHOPPING
BAG

OKIKU SAN

alike, both wearing kimonos and obis. The girl's kimono will be brighter, her obi will be wider. A boy's kimono has a smaller printed design. His obi is narrow and it is tied in a simple knot, with short ends.

O-Kiku-San's kimono requires a bit of flowery silk 7 by 14 inches. When folded for cutting it will be exactly square. An opening is cut down the center of the front. The pattern page shows where the seams are to be taken. Notice that each sleeve is to be left open along the inside but is closed along the outside except the rather wide opening for the doll's hand.

Kimono material doesn't actually have to be silk, for soft cotton stuff will work up much better than a stiff silk. Stiffish materials will bunch up and look bulky on the doll. The goods does not have to be in a floral pattern, either, though you will probably like floral effects best. Sometimes we make a kimono of striped cotton, with a plain obi. One we made of plain cotton in a rosy shade, and with this we combined an obi of deep, rich coloring.

Much of the beauty of Japanese dress lies in its lovely color and design. Big, splashy designs are often used in all the gorgeous colors you can think of. Small, careful de-

OPEN

OPEN

KIMONO

ON FOLD

7 INCHES WIDE

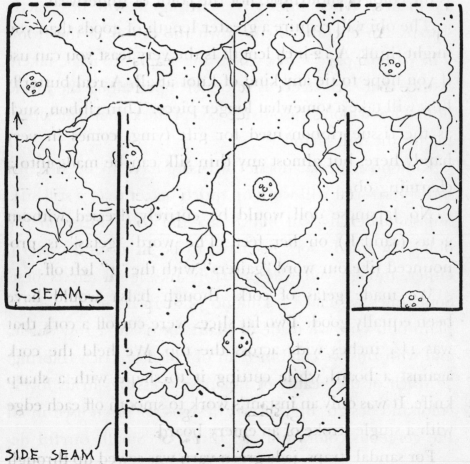

SEAM →

↑

SIDE SEAM

signs are also worn, especially by men and boys. Stripes, too. Even plaids sometimes!

We did not illustrate an underdress for Kiku, but it is a kimono just like the outer one except that it has no sleeves. But do not make it of white goods! In Japan, white is the color of mourning, not the color of underwear.

The obi will require a greater length of goods than you might think. A 12-inch length is the very least you can use if you hope to tie any kind of knot at all. A real butterfly bow will take a somewhat longer piece. Thin ribbon, such as the tissue ribbon used for gift tying, comes in very handy here, but almost any thin silk can be made into a charming obi.

No Japanese doll would be entirely dressed without getas (sandals) on her feet. The word "getas" is pronounced like our word "gaiters" with the "r" left off.

We made getas of cork, though balsa would have been equally good. Two fat slices were cut off a cork that was 1½ inches wide across the top. We held the cork against a board while cutting it to shape with a sharp knife. It was only an instant's work to smooth off each edge with a single stroke of an emery board.

For sandal straps, jade green yarn was sewed up through

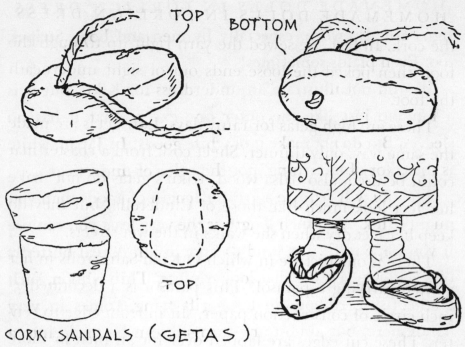

TOP

BOTTOM

TOP

CORK SANDALS (GETAS)

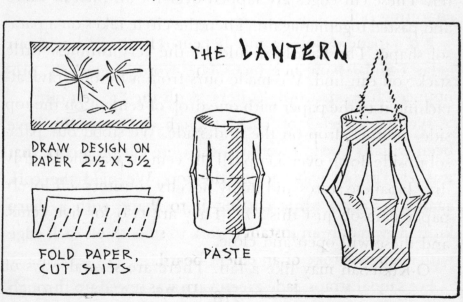

THE **LANTERN**

DRAW DESIGN ON
PAPER 2½ X 3½

FOLD PAPER,
CUT SLITS

PASTE

the cork. In fact, we sewed the yarn right up through the foot, then poked the loose ends out of sight underneath the foot.

These are high getas for rainy days. Low getas are made the same way, only thinner. Sheet cork from a coaster mat could be used, also balsa wood. Kiku's getas do not make her feet look much like those of Cinderella, but they do keep her feet dry when she walks in the wet streets.

There is one picture in which O-Kiku-San strolls in her garden carrying a parasol. This parasol is a decorated 5-inch circle of construction paper, slit in from edge to center. These cut edges are lapped over for an inch or more and pasted together again. Then the circle takes on a parasol shape. The handle should be the very thinnest little stick you can find. We made ours from a broomstraw, attaching it to the paper with one drop of cement on the top side, another drop on the underside. We stood our parasol upside down over a cup till the cement was thoroughly dry. Japanese stores and many novelty counters sell lovely paper parasols just this size. They are two for five cents, and these will open and close.

O-Kiku-San may like a fan. There are several ways of

making a midget paper fan for Kiku to hold in her hand. But the easiest kind we know of is made of a fluted paper candy cup, the kind that holds a single bonbon. Flatten the cup, fold it across the center, then fold it again into one quarter of its former size. Presto! A fan! Kiku's hand can be bent to hold it, or you can pin it on. There should be a few dashes of color on the fan.

O-Kiku-San must have a home she can call her own. This home will have paper windows. Most Japanese houses have windows of tough linen paper instead of glass. Earthquakes can shake a glass window to pieces, but they don't harm a paper window of this kind.

IMPORTANT POINTS TO REMEMBER in making the house:

The roof is very wide.

Windows are not all the same size.

Even window panes are of different sizes and shapes.

There is always a shoe-off place outside the door.

Our house was made of a corrugated carton, its roof of corrugated board with one side ridged. The carton was 11 inches wide, 8 inches deep and 11 inches high. We cut the

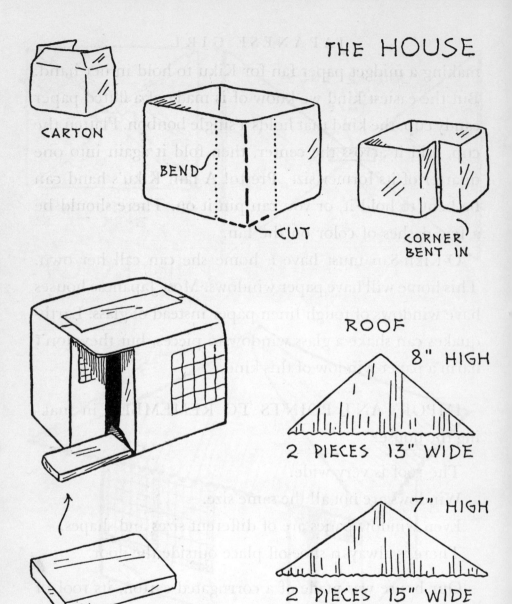

THE HOUSE

CARTON

BEND

CUT

CORNER
BENT IN

ROOF

8" HIGH

2 PIECES 13" WIDE

7" HIGH

2 PIECES 15" WIDE

BOX LID FOR
"SHOE-OFF PLACE"

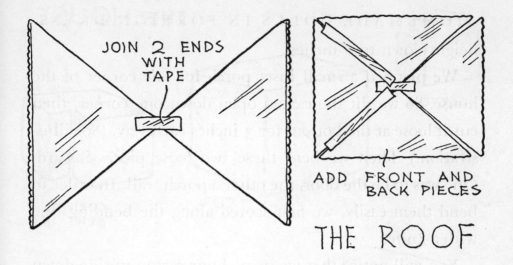

JOIN 2 ENDS WITH TAPE

ADD FRONT AND BACK PIECES

THE ROOF

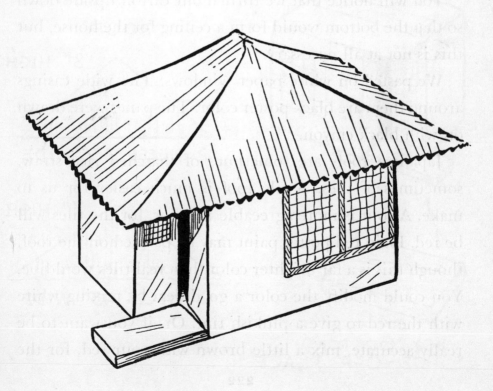

height down to 8 inches.

We planned a small inset porch for one corner of the house. So we slit the carton open down one corner, then cut it loose at the bottom for 3 inches each way. (See illustration.) Then we bent these two loose pieces inward. One was to be the door, the other a porch wall. In order to bend them easily, we first scored along the bending line with a knife.

You will notice that we turned our carton upside down so that the bottom would form a ceiling for the house, but this is not at all necessary.

We pasted on white paper windows. The wide casings around them are black poster color. The panes were drawn on with black crayon.

Japanese roofs are sometimes of thatched rice straw, sometimes of tiles. A tile roof is much easier for us to make. Also it is more agreeable in color, for the tiles will be red. Plain red poster paint may be painted on the roof, though this is a far brighter color than real tiles would be. You could modify the color a good deal by mixing white with the red to give a pinkish tint. Or, if you want to be really accurate, mix a little brown with your red, for the real tiles are a rather dull, brownish red. This painting should be done *before* the roof pieces are joined together.

The roof is made in four pieces—two end pieces, two side pieces—all cut from corrugated board. End pieces are 8 by 13 inches. The other two pieces will be 7 by 15 inches. The joining is done on the smooth under side, and is done with gummed paper tape. Cloth tape is excellent, if you happen to have it. But even gummed envelope flaps will do the work if no tape is at hand.

We found it convenient to connect the two end pieces together first. Then we added the other two pieces in the way shown in one of the illustrations.

The hardest part is the joining of that last corner. For when you draw the two last edges together, the roof humps up into its pointed shape instead of lying flat as it does up to that time. But even this part of it isn't really hard; just prop it up against something, lay weights where needed to hold it steady for pasting, and leave it propped up till it is perfectly dry.

Everyone knows that the cleanly Japanese take off their sandals before entering the house, just as we would take off our muddy overshoes. So each home has a sort of wide doorstep called the "shoe-off place." Sometimes it is as large as a small porch.

The shoe-off place in our illustration of the house happens to be a small green board that once held thumbtacks. For another house we set up a small box lid. Next time we'll try a cigar box lid and see how it looks. The paper must be soaked off, of course. It is fun to try out new ways of doing things instead of always doing them in the same old way. Every once in a while you stumble on a fine, new discovery.

In case you can't conveniently lay hands on an 8 by 11-inch carton, there's a quick and easy way of making a substitute house of the same dimensions. This house is not nearly as solid as the other, but the same roof will fit it. Once you see how attractive a Japanese house can be, we think you will keep on the lookout for a carton suitable for constructing the house as we first described it.

The small illustrations show how to make the substitute house out of three shirt cardboards. When laid sidewise, as shown, the cardboards are the right height for the house walls. You merely lap and fasten the three pieces together, there's no cutting at all.

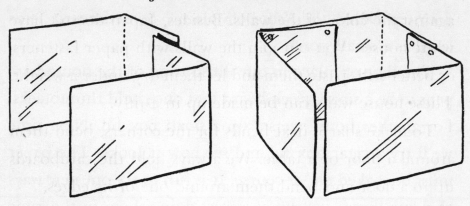

SUBSTITUTE HOUSE of SHIRT CARDBOARDS

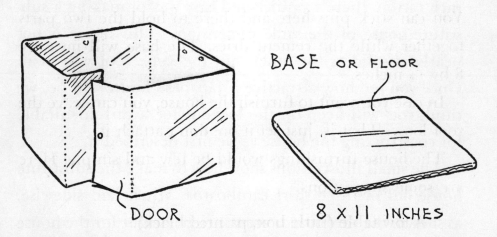

DOOR

BASE OR FLOOR

8 x 11 INCHES

It is best to put the gray side of the board out, not the white side. You want the white paper windows to show up

225

against the color of the walls. Besides, Japan doesn't have white houses. You can join the walls with paper fasteners, or better still, paste them and let them dry under a weight. These house walls can be made up in a jiffy.

To make sharp, neat bends for the corners, bend them around a door or a table. We always hold the cardboards up to a door and bend them around one of its edges.

This cardboard house will have more firmness if you set its walls over a base which is cut from a stiff piece of carton board. What we really mean is to set the walls *around* the base, then cement the lower wall edges to it. You can stick pins here and there to hold the two parts together while the cement dries. The base will measure 8 by 11 inches.

In case you want to furnish the house, you can leave the roof loose. That is, just set it on, don't attach it.

The house furnishings would be few and simple. Here are some suggestions:

A low table (little box, painted black).
Acorn-cup bowls (for tea parties).
Flat mats (for visiting dolls to sit on).

Flowers (set into a spool or cork).

Folding screen (decorated paper or cardboard).

Ornamented scrolls (to hang on the wall).

No house would be home to a Japanese doll unless it had a garden and a pool, for in that green and pleasant land there are gardens everywhere.

When you say "Japanese garden," the first thing everyone thinks of is blossoming cherry trees. And these need not be at all hard to make. Twigs, real ones, dipped in wet starch or thin glue can be sprinkled with shreds of pink Kleenex or tissue paper. A few minutes' work would provide you with a whole cherry orchard, all pink and blooming.

When the setting is arranged on a sand table, or on a sand box in the game room or some such place, there are many delightful ways of adding to it. You can even have tiny live goldfish in a low bowl, such as a Pyrex dish with blue paper under it. Stones, moss, etc., could be banked up around to hide the bowl itself.

Another way of making a pool is to lay a piece of glass over blue blotter or paper. Even part of a broken mirror

227

would make a gleaming pool which would reflect the scenery around it. You could arrange green modeling clay, or pebbles and dried moss, or shells to hide the edges of the glass. Cut out green lily pads and pink or white water lilies to lay on top of the glass here and there.

Small potted plants add much to a Japanese garden. Or larger plants, for that matter. A fern or a geranium would look like a tree beside O-Kiku-San. A bamboo grove could be made of slender bamboo plant sticks rigged out with fringy paper branches at the top. These bamboo trees would be planted close together in the sand or soil of the sand box.

You must have many flowers in the garden, for Japan is the Flowery Kingdom. The irises we show are green-colored toothpicks with paper petals. Two shades of purple crepe paper made the blossoms. Other colors of iris could be made, as well as any other flowers you like. Strangely enough, the Japanese do not prize roses as we do. They do not think them beautiful because of the thorns.

One of those graceful, curved bridges would fit in well. Materials for the bridge: balloon sticks, rattan, or reeds softened in hot water and bent while still wet; cardboard

floor with split twigs cemented to it; joints to be cemented rather than glued. Use airplane cement, or any good household cement similar to Duco.

MORE THINGS TO MAKE: Miniature paper lanterns (illustrated). Attach a thread handle to each lantern. Hang lanterns from the eaves of the house or in festoons across the garden. Tie one to a stick and put it in Kiku's hand, as we did.

Torii (or gateways); a ricksha; and last of all, Fujiyama with its snowy peak.

If your setting allows suitable space for a background, by all means make Fujiyama, Japan's sacred mountain. This has been called the most beautiful mountain on earth, and perhaps it is. At any rate, we could make a fine cutout poster of it to hang on the wall behind a sand table setting. The cardboard shape could either be painted with poster paint, or it could have colored paper cut-outs pasted on.

To make the mountain look far away, make the lower part a dim blue or purple. The stronger the color is, the closer Fuji will appear. The more grayish and pale the colors, the more distant will Fuji seem to be.

AFRICAN JUNGLE BOY

GUMBO lives in the Congo. The setting shows Gumbo's hut and two palm trees (whose construction is explained in the Arabian chapter).

From behind the hut Gumbo peers with inquisitive eyes. He has left his shield leaning against the hut. The tomtom stands nearby. We can change this scene as we like. For instance, we could stand Gumbo in a dancing pose and let him have a jubilee all by himself.

When Gumbo dances, he has with him all his dearest treasures. There will be his spear and shield, armlets and anklets, and, best of all, his tiger claw necklace. He wears that for luck.

The tiger claws are muskmelon seeds strung on a thread. Grains of puffed rice can be used in place of seeds. Circular paper clips, bone curtain rings, or assorted beads make

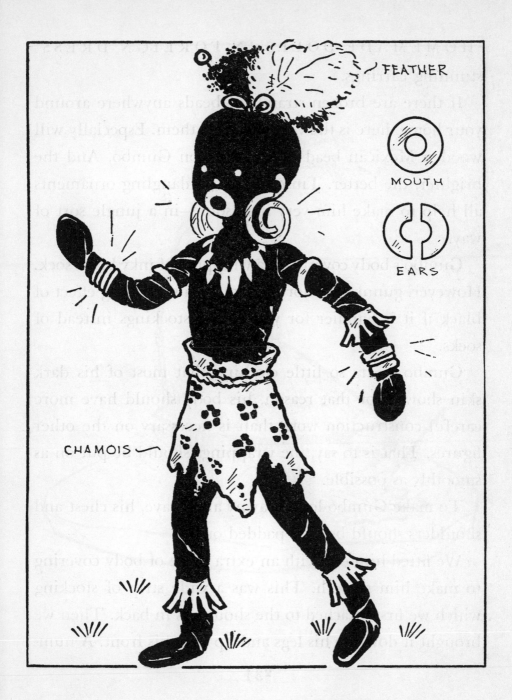

FEATHER

MOUTH

EARS

CHAMOIS

stunning earrings.

If there are broken strands of beads anywhere around your home, here is the very place for them. Especially will wooden Mexican beads look grand on Gumbo. And the brighter, the better. Tinsel cord and dangling ornaments all help to make him very handsome—in a jungle sort of way.

Gumbo's body covering is a wrapping of inky black sock. However, gunmetal color gives quite a surprising effect of black if it is handier for you to use stockings instead of socks.

Gumbo wears so little clothing that most of his dark skin shows. For that reason, his body should have more careful construction work than is necessary on the other figures. That is to say, the wrappings should be put on as smoothly as possible.

To make Gumbo look brawny and brave, his chest and shoulders should be well padded out.

We fitted him out with an extra piece of body covering to make him smooth. This was a wide strip of stocking which we first attached to the shoulders in back. Then we brought it down to his legs and up over his front. A num-

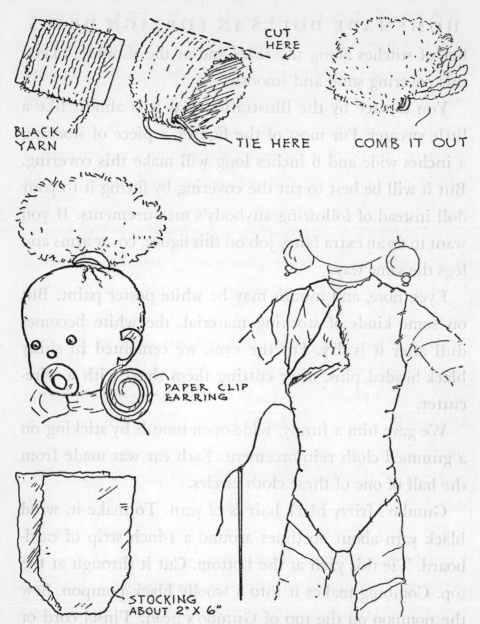

BLACK YARN

CUT HERE

TIE HERE

COMB IT OUT

PAPER CLIP EARRING

STOCKING ABOUT 2" X 6"

FIT A SMOOTH NEW COVERING AROUND BODY

ber of stitches along the sides and at the shoulders keep this covering snug and smooth.

You can see by the illustration that it is almost like a little sweater. For most of the figures, a piece of stocking 2 inches wide and 6 inches long will make this covering. But it will be best to cut the covering by fitting it to your doll instead of following anybody's measurements. If you want to do an extra fancy job on this figure, cover arms and legs the same way.

Eyes, nose, and mouth may be white poster paint. But on some kinds of stocking material, the white becomes dull after it is dry. For the eyes, we cemented in shiny black-headed pins, after cutting them short with a wire-cutter.

We gave him a funny, wide-open mouth by sticking on a gummed cloth reinforcement. Each ear was made from the half of one of these cloth circles.

Gumbo's frizzy black hair is of yarn. To make it, wind black yarn about 20 times around a 1-inch strip of cardboard. Tie this yarn at the bottom. Cut it through at the top. Combing makes it into a woolly black pompon. Sew the pompon on the top of Gumbo's head. Tinsel cord or some bright thread wrapped around the knotted part will make the hair stand up in a magnificent tuft. You can then ornament the topknot with whatever colored pins, beads, or feathers you can gather up.

As to clothes, let him wear a leopard skin. A leopard skin would be a trophy of the hunt, and Gumbo is supposed to be a mighty hunter of Darkest Africa.

The leopard skin can be chamois or yellow cloth on which you paint black dots in clusters of five. Make it wide enough to wrap around his waist and lap over a little. Tie it on with a cord in some brave color, such as fiery scarlet. Cut the bottom of this robe so it is uneven just as a real leopard skin would be.

SPEAR. Gumbo must have a spear of some kind. In the jungle they say that a man without a spear is only half a man. A steel knitting needle makes the finest of spears. Just pinch Gumbo's little black hand around it. This spear shines beautifully.

Or you can insert a paper spear-head into the slit end of a piece of balloon stick for a spear. You would then wrap string decoration somewhere on its shaft. The stick would be perhaps 10 inches long or so.

SHIELD. A shield may be any size from 3 to 5 inches long. It should be painted in the most barbarous colors you can think of. But use white, too. It helps make the other colors look brighter.

Materials for shield may be leather, cardboard, or paper. For one, we used a piece of leather from an old brown billfold.

We made another shield from bright green construction paper, with splashes of white and black paint on it. (See illustration.) But remember, every tribesman paints his own shield in his own design. And you can do the same.

As an arm strap for the shield, try using a rubber band. Push its two end loops through two holes in the shield. The loops come out at the back of the shield so they can be slipped over Gumbo's wrist.

The base on which Gumbo stands is a paper saucer. If you perch him up on one dancing foot, this foot must be strongly attached to the base. Fasten it in two or more places.

When the figure is arranged as you want it, the base can be concealed under a sprinkling of sand or gravel. Green modeling clay is good for this, too.

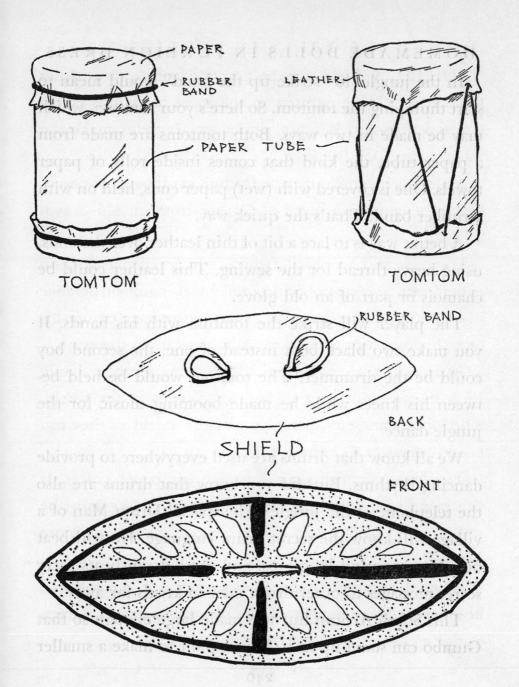

PAPER

RUBBER
BAND

PAPER TUBE

LEATHER

TOMTOM

TOMTOM

RUBBER BAND

SHIELD

BACK

FRONT

In the jungle, to "strike up the band" would mean to start thumping the tomtom. So here's your tomtom, which may be made in two ways. Both tomtoms are made from a paper tube, the kind that comes inside rolls of paper towels. One is covered with (wet) paper ends, held on with a rubber band. That's the quick way.

A better way is to lace a bit of thin leather over the ends, using heavy thread for the sewing. This leather could be chamois or part of an old glove.

The player will strike the tomtom with his hands. If you make two black boys instead of one, the second boy could be the drummer. The tomtom would be held between his knees while he made booming music for the jungle dance.

We all know that drums are used everywhere to provide dancing rhythms. But did you know that drums are also the telephone of the jungle? The special Drum Man of a village will know the secret drum language. He will beat out short taps and long taps, and these drum beats carry secret messages to other drum men in kraals far away.

This South African hut was made large enough so that Gumbo can stand up in it. If you want to make a smaller

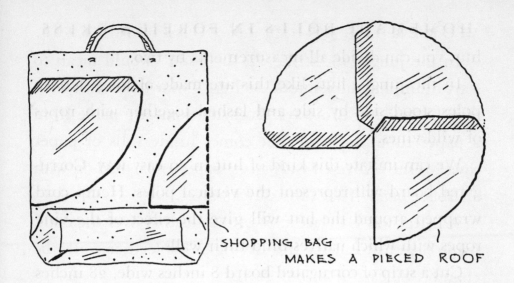

SHOPPING BAG
MAKES A PIECED ROOF

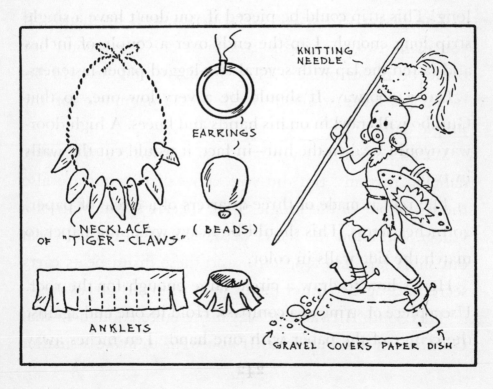

EARRINGS

KNITTING
NEEDLE

NECKLACE
OF "TIGER-CLAWS"

(BEADS)

ANKLETS

GRAVEL COVERS PAPER DISH

hut, you can divide all measurements by two.

In the jungle, huts like this are made of long slender poles stood side by side and lashed together with ropes of wild vines.

We can imitate this kind of hut in an easy way. Corrugated board will represent the vertical poles. Hemp cord wrapped around the hut will give the effect of the vine ropes with which natives bind their walls.

Cut a strip of corrugated board 8 inches wide, 28 inches long. This strip could be pieced if you don't have a single strip long enough. Lap the ends over a couple of inches and fasten the lap with several two-legged paper fasteners.

Cut a doorway. It should be a very low one, so that Gumbo will crawl in on his hands and knees. A high doorway would weaken the hut—in fact, it would cut the walls in two!

The roof is made of three-quarters of a circle of paper, 20 inches across. This should be heavy wrapping paper to match the side walls in color.

Here's how to draw a circle large enough for the roof. Use a piece of string as a compass. Hold its one end against the center of the paper with one hand. Ten inches away

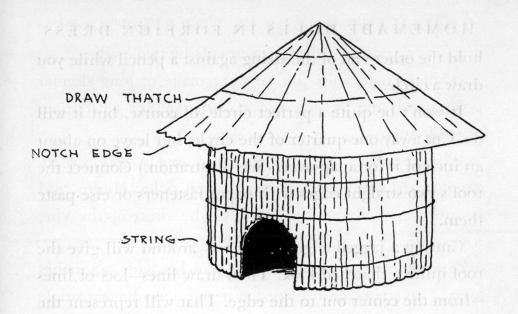

DRAW THATCH

NOTCH EDGE

STRING

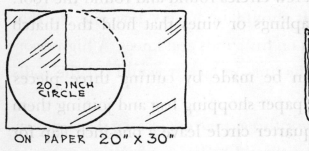

20-INCH
CIRCLE

ON PAPER 20" X 30"

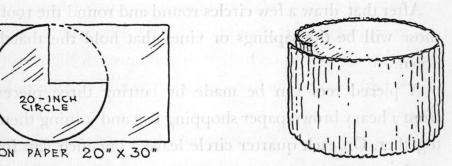

CORRUGATED BOARD
8 INCHES WIDE
28 INCHES LONG

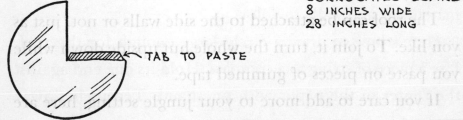

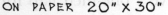

TAB TO PASTE

hold the other end of the string against a pencil while you draw a circle.

It won't be quite a perfect circle, of course, but it will do. Cut away one-quarter of the circle, but leave on about an inch of it for a lap-over. (See illustration.) Connect the roof's two straight edges with paper fasteners or else paste them.

Cutting a jagged edge all the way around will give the roof quite a thatched look. Then draw lines—lots of lines —from the center out to the edge. That will represent the long grasses.

After that, draw a few circles round and round the roof; those will be the saplings or vines that hold the thatch down.

A pieced roof can be made by cutting three pieces from a heavy brown paper shopping bag and joining them together. On each quarter circle leave a one-inch flap for pasting.

The roof can be attached to the side walls or not, just as you like. To join it, turn the whole hut upside down while you paste on pieces of gummed tape.

If you care to add more to your jungle setting, here are

suggestions:

Ceremonial masks, feather headdresses.

Outrigger and dugout canoes.

Ivory tusks (of whittled sticks, or pieces of parsnip or
potato—stand them against the hut).

Calabash gourds (of peanut shell).

Stockade fence for the kraal.

The African word "kraal" sounds like our American
word "corral." And it means the same, too, for a kraal is a
pen for cattle. But in Africa, kraal also means a village inside a stockade fence. This stockade is built exactly as our
early Americans built stockade fences around forts in Indian days.

You can make the stockade from the same kind of corrugated board as the hut. Then arrange your setting inside
it, with the hut, palm trees, shrubs, and Gumbo.

You can make up one of these figures as the beloved
little Black Sambo. You need only dress him in a beautiful little red coat and beautiful little blue trousers and
beautiful little purple shoes with crimson linings. If he
should want a green umbrella, he could have one made

HOMEMADE DOLLS IN FOREIGN DRESS

like O-Kiku-San's in the Japanese chapter.

There are even tigers waiting to be made! A tiger's body would be an inch longer than the burro's in the Mexican chapter and he'd be covered with yellow instead of black. Otherwise the general construction would be the same.